NOT ENOUGH ROOM
to swing a cat

NAVAL SLANG AND ITS EVERYDAY USAGE

Martin Robson
Illustrations by Mark Myers

CONWAY

A Conway Maritime Book

© Martin Robson, 2008
© illustrations, Mark Myers, 2008

First published in Great Britain in 2008 by Conway
an imprint of Anova Books Company Ltd
10 Southcombe Street
London W14 0RA
www.conwaypublishing.com

Reprinted 2009, 2010

Front cover image © National Maritime Museum, Greenwich (D3920)

British Library Cataloguing in Publication Data
A catalogue record for this book is available from the British Library

ISBN 9781844860739

Printed by Bookwell, Finland

To receive regular email updates on forthcoming Conway titles, email conway@anovabooks.com with Conway Update in the subject field.

Contents

ACKNOWLEDGEMENTS

With a remarkable sense of timing, in the middle of writing this book I moved house from the North East of England to the South West. After this hiatus I found myself desperately in need of an Internet connection and (with my supposed study a chaotic jumble of book boxes piled on top of one another) a place to sit down and work. Help came in the form of the local pub. I owe a huge debt of gratitude to Tony Stearman, landlord of The Poachers Inn, Ide, and all his kind staff. Not only did they allow me to make extensive use of their wireless broadband and electricity, they also allowed me to turn one corner of the pub into a library/office from which I worked on this book for several weeks. As well as tolerating my working habits, they also kept me supplied with a steady supply of rather fine ales (though I must admit failing to match the ration of eight pints a day sailors in Nelson's time consumed).

I must also thank my friends and former colleagues at Conway Maritime Press. John Lee, Publisher, was a keen supporter of this project from the start and provided some excellent and knowledgeable comments and suggestions. Project Manager, Alison Moss, provided splendid editorial support. Both displayed a remarkable degree of patience and tolerance when I had to put down my pen for a number of weeks to move house. Thanks are also due to Mark Myers: his skilful and witty illustrations provide a splendid visual accompaniment to the text. The Royal Navy granted me permission to reproduce excerpts from Covey Crump's work on naval slang and other content from their website (www.royal-navy.mod.uk) for which I am extremely grateful.

My mother and father have provided support and encouragement throughout my chosen career; I owe them more thanks than I can ever elucidate. Last, but certainly not least, I must thank Charlotte; a source of constant inspiration. Not only did she read the first drafts, commenting, suggesting, proofing and editing some of my more convoluted syntax, she also posed some awkward, but necessary questions. Her input has certainly made this a far better book; of course, any errors that remain in the text are entirely my own. It is to Charlotte that this book is dedicated.

Martin Robson

INTRODUCTION

During the writing of this book one question kept coming up: why write another book on naval slang when there are others on the subject already out there? I admit, there are a number of fine books already published that have looked at naval slang. Some of these have even proved useful in writing this book. If that's the case, does the world need another volume on naval slang?

Most of the books that look at naval slang do so in alphabetical order. Rick Jolly's *Jackspeak* and Peter Jeans' *Ship to Shore* are organised in this way, which makes them great works of reference, though perhaps not great reading books. Moreover, *Jackspeak* is specifically aimed at current and ex-service personnel; much of the content within is limited in use to those afloat, while many of the entries in *Ship to Shore* do not contain contextual material linking them to modern society.

Readers hoping to find an exhaustive dictionary of all slang terms here will be disappointed. I make no apologies for that: what I am interested in are terms that have passed from 'Jack Tar' to the 'landlubbers' ashore. Even within that limited remit many words and phrases have been omitted; perhaps the chance will come to write a second volume (readers who do find their favourite slang terms missing can send suggestions to the publishers at the relevant address).

What this book does is plant naval slang terms squarely in our everyday existence. I have found naval terms used ashore today in familiar places: war films, newspapers and naval fiction. But naval slang crops up in some unexpected places. From US Presidential speeches to the ramblings of a drunken cartoon robot, words and phrases that originated at sea are all around us: we just need to open our eyes and ears to them. In fact many people today will use naval slang and not even realise it. I hope that this book goes some way towards remedying this situation.

This book is organised by subject matter, thereby placing the words and phrases in context surrounded by other words and phrases dealing with a similar subject. Some entries are interrelated, others stand alone. For instance, readers will find everything relating to food, or 'munjy', together. Introducing each chapter is a section contextualising the entries that follow; using 'munjy' as the example again, readers will find out what sailors from different periods of time actually ate before going on to look at some of the related phrases in depth. I hope this approach will provide readers with a more rounded experience and understanding of naval slang and will add to, rather than replicate, the literature that already exists.

I have defined slang as any type of informal language used to describe things, activities or circumstances. Quite often slang is a quicker way of saying something or making reference to something. Naval slang is of particular interest in this case as many activities that were undertaken on board a ship had to be done quickly and accurately by sailors; their lives sometimes depended on it. So their language was, and still is, an organic entity, it ebbs and flows like the tide. Some words and phrases appear and fall out of use, only to reappear at a future point in time, sometimes in a completely different context.

A great deal of naval slang comes from the classic age of the sailing man-of-war, roughly 1600–1850, and originated in the Royal Navy. This is not really surprising; it was an age of war, with Britain engaged in a series of conflicts with France, Spain and the newly independent United States – all flexing their maritime muscles at different times. Where possible I have stated where the use of words can be traced to a specific country; for example 'Gung Ho' originated in China and was picked up by the US Marine Corps.

As maritime trade and empires rose and fell, the sailor's vocabulary expanded. Naval slang was once the preserve of the sailor – an incomprehensible language culled from the four corners of the world. The words the sailor picked up, perhaps from Arabic, Old Scandinavian, or even Mandarin Chinese, were employed afloat and brought back to port with him. The subsequent transfer ashore of such words was inevitable, given the contact between sailors and landlubbers in ports across the world and the portrayal of the navy in wider popular culture.

Alongside the geographic expansion, in times of war, when large numbers of men (and in the twentieth century, women) were mobilised in service, naval traditions and language became a shared experience for many. By the end of the Second World War the Royal Navy could boast 866,000 enlisted men and women. The reintroduction of such huge numbers of people back into life ashore after this and other conflicts helped to spread naval slang in the decades following major conflicts.

A short essay examining shore-based perceptions of the sailor has been included as an Appendix.

If this book can do one thing, I hope it helps to show that, as much as the sea can be perceived as a barrier, it can also act as highway, bringing people together and helping to spread ideas, words, phrases and experiences.

A Final Word Of Caution

Of course, some of the terms and words used by sailors fall under that category we might call swearing: i.e. rude, offensive or sexist. In order to provide some examples of the way sailors have often thought of the world around them I have collected a sample of these towards the end of Chapter 9 – Poking Charlie. If you think they might shock or offend you, then you don't have to look.

1

ALL SHIPSHAPE AND BRISTOL FASHION

From the mighty aircraft carrier to the tiny midget submarine, without ships there would be no navies, no sailors and no naval slang.

Building a navy is an expensive undertaking. For some countries such as Britain and the United States, the navy was, and in some cases still is, a symbol of state power – an instrument with which to influence world events. For other states, naval vessels are a luxury – and can be a source of conflict rather than a safeguard. Throughout history man has interacted with the sea. Ever since seafaring people such as the Phoenicians took to the seas to trade there have been battles at sea and hence the need for specialised fighting vessels. Initially, such ships could combine the duties of a merchantman and a warship but eventually the two needs could only be addressed by diversification, thereby giving the world the man-of-war. Navies serve many purposes: they protect territorial water, they protect maritime trade and they allow a state to project force over a wide area. Navies can influence wars on land, whether by direct action (bombardment or landing troops) or by more subtle means (cutting supply lines and blockading ports). However, different roles require different ships, and different ships need different designs if they are to fulfil their roles adequately.

So what makes a warship a warship? Well, obviously there is some form of offensive capability. This could be just using the ship as a weapon, like the ancient galleys equipped with a ram; it could carry fighting men; or, and this is what most people are familiar with, it could carry offensive weapons systems – cannon, missiles and torpedoes. Warships also need protection, and they need to be stable, safe and habitable. Those who have designed vessels for war have always tried to solve a unique puzzle: namely how to balance carrying offensive armament while retaining a defensive capability, to be seaworthy and provide accommodation for the crew.

Throughout history there are numerous instances of massive loss of life due to some flaw in warship design. Just a couple of examples will show what can happen when a ship design is not 'A1'. Naval disasters are not new; during the First Punic War (264–241 BC) against Carthage, Rome had two fleets virtually wiped out because of their inherent instability in bad weather, losing around 200,000 men in the process. Another tragic example occurred in 1870: while cruising off Cape Finisterre the Royal Navy's HMS *Captain* overturned and went to the bottom taking with her 500 men and her inventor, Captain Cowper Coles. Coles had tried to combine a new technology of guns housed in turrets with an old-style sailing rig. The result was a top-heavy, unstable ship and this caused the disaster that cost so many men their lives. More recent tragedies include the Russian Federation Submarine *Kursk*, which was lost with 118 men due to faulty torpedoes in August 2000.

Warships have many component parts, from the depths of the hull, through the many and varied decks, to the necessary propulsion (whether that be sails or engines) and each has a role to play. It should be remembered the ship is more than just an instrument of war; it is where men live, and sometimes die, in the service of their country. Naturally, the sailor has a love-hate relationship with the ships he serves on. His very existence depends on the safe construction and fitting of his warship. Many have successfully matched the needs of such design issues, others have not. On occasion the sailor has been let down, either by ill-thought-out designs or by the pressure applied by bureaucrats to keep the costs down. Such waters provide much inspiration for that sailor to apply his inimitable view of the world around him to the colourful language of the sea.

A1

The term 'A1' is often used to describe something that is, or was, good or excellent. For instance, 'that burger I had last night was A1'. It is also a common name for modern business ventures that want to give the impression of being the best in their particular field. In the UK it is particularly favoured by many mini cab firms and Chinese Takeaways that want to appear on the first page of local print or Internet business listings. The term has also had widespread use across the globe, from a 1933 Nazi rocket design and a Macedonian TV station, to an Anglo-Norwegian boy band and an American brand of steak sauce. (The infamous A1 in northern England is certainly not an 'A1'-standard road.)

The original term 'A1' refers to the certificates of seaworthiness as awarded by Lloyd's Register of Shipping. Edward Lloyd's coffee house served as the hub for maritime and shipping gossip in late seventeenth-century London. Ever the entrepreneur, Lloyd decided to use this gossip to produce a news sheet which was eventually formalised with the founding of the Register Society in 1760. The first official *Register of Ships* was printed in 1764 and contained the details of 4,500 ships. The Register consisted of a classification system which would make an assessment of the actual physical state of sailing ships. This system allowed merchants and insurance underwriters to make informed judgements as to hiring, chartering and insuring the ships in question.

The condition of a ship's hull was classified by the letters A, E, I, O, U, with A being the best category. Equipment such as rigging, sails, masts, anchors and so on, was initially classified with the letters G (good), M (middling) or B (bad). This classification was replaced in 1768–9 by lower case letters for the hulls and numbers for the fittings, with 1 being the best category. The letters were then changed back to upper case, giving the world the famous description '**A1 at Lloyd's**'. Insurers and merchants would know that any ship categorised as such would be in the very best possible condition. Of course, the wily sailor has often applied the Lloyd's system to other areas, as Midshipman Alexander Scrimgeour of HMS *Invincible* observed in 1915:

> *Yesterday I went to tea with Mrs Hood and family; they have a house on shore near our base, with a tennis court and some excellent strawberry beds. As there are two A1 daughters of seventeen and nineteen, you can bet their hospitality is fully appreciated.*

All above board

> *'Well, sir, you have been fair-spoken to me, though I can see that I have you to thank that I have these bracelets upon my wrists. Still, I bear no grudge for that. It is all fair and above board.'*
> Jonathon Small, *The Sign of Four* by Arthur Conan Doyle

The term 'all above board' is frequently used to describe fair play, and often appears in reference to business dealings or a legitimate venture. The word 'board' is possibly from the Anglo-Saxon *bord*, relating to the planks used to construct the sides of a ship. Therefore, all above board was the term used to describe all the parts of a ship above the deck, i.e. all that was visible of the ship to an observer.

Another possible origin of the term was from the practice of captains, when entering combat, using the fiendish ruse of keeping some of their men below decks, i.e. '**below boards**', so that the enemy could not know the true strength of the crew.

Other sources indicate that the term might derive from gaming and card tables where players were encouraged to keep their hands in view above the table (board), thereby preventing some of the shadier practices that could occur under the table.

Awash

Nowadays, people often think that to be awash with something is a good thing. Headlines scream of people and places being awash with things: companies awash with cash, countries awash with oil and so on. The *Independent on Sunday* on 14 October 2007 proudly stated, 'The emerging economies are awash with money'. This meaning could not be further from its origins.

If a sailor found his ship awash he would be very worried indeed, for to be 'awash' is to be covered in water. The term refers to the precise moment when a ship becomes so submerged that its decks become awash with water. Clearly in this state the ship and all those on her are in extreme danger, unless the vessel in question is a submarine, in which case to be awash is a common situation where the boat sits in the water perfectly safe with water washing across her decks. This word is not to be confused with the small Ethiopian town of the same name that sits on the River Awash.

Cold enough to freeze the balls off a brass monkey

> *There is something slightly immature about using a rugby match to air centuries-old grievances, and the Scots were at it again at Murrayfield as England ran out to be confronted by a group of torch-brandishing dervishes dressed in extra's outfits from the set of* **Braveheart***. Had it not been cold enough to reconfigure the nether regions of a brass monkey, they would probably have bent over – William Wallace style – to let the visitors know that a true Scot neither cares much for the English, nor wears much under his kilt.*
>
> Martin Johnson, *Telegraph*, 27 February 2006

This colloquial phrase, as employed rather inventively by England's Rugby World Cup-winning captain in the quote above, is commonly used in the UK to describe extreme cold weather. According to much repeated orthodox naval tradition, a limited supply of four cannonballs was stored on ship next to each gun so as to be ready for immediate action. The balls were stacked up in pyramid fashion, a brass plate or tray (the monkey) incorporating three rings into which three balls were stacked, with the fourth ball sitting on the top. When, in extremely cold conditions, the brass contracted faster than the iron balls, the weight of the top ball would push the lower three off the plate sending them rolling across the deck. This was a very worrying prospect considering the amount of cannon carried by ships in the age of sail. For example at the Battle of Trafalgar, HMS *Victory*, a first rate ship of 100 guns, carried thirty '32 pounders' just on her main gun deck.

Other sources point to the brass cannon, nicknamed a 'monkey', of seventeenth-century warships. Again, cold weather would make the brass contract faster than the iron cannonballs, thereby creating too much windage (the gap between the ball and the cannon chamber) for the cannon to shoot. In this interpretation the phrase is worded to freeze the balls *of* a brass monkey rather than *off* a brass monkey.

Another interpretation has Oriental entrepreneurs cashing in on the influx of western visitors in the nineteenth and twentieth centuries by casting and selling small brass monkey souvenirs of the Three Wise Monkeys at the Toshogu Shrine in Nikko, Japan. Some included a fourth monkey who used his hands to cover his modesty. Moreover, the phrase **'freeze the tail off a brass monkey'** seems to have originated in the United States during the 1850s and supports the theory of substandard oriental manufacturing practices at that time leading to problems with brass monkey souvenirs in inclement conditions.

Shipshape and Bristol fashion

British journalists were typically excited in May 2005 when a story appeared that combined two of their favourite subjects; political correctness gone mad and local government. The story claimed that local councillors in Bristol had been told by 'equality and diversity experts' not to use the phrase 'all ship shape and Bristol fashion' due to its racist connotations regarding the selling of slaves. In fact, there was little evidence that the 'experts' had actually made the statement. This minor oversight did not prevent an article 'Thought Police Go Overboard' appearing in the *Telegraph,* while the Lord Mayor of Bristol, Peter Abraham, volleyed back, 'I have used the term for 60 years and my family has and there is no way it can be regarded as politically incorrect.'

Well, despite the best attempts of the press to blow up the story, the Lord Mayor was correct. The term actually refers to the reputation for ships operating out of the West Country port to be well handled and kept neat and tidy: 'shipshape'. Moreover, due to the fact that Bristol sits inland on the River Avon, which has a large tidal range, ships would become beached at every low tide. Not only did they have to be built strong enough to withstand this unusual buffeting, but all the goods, equipment and material on board had to be securely stowed to prevent objects moving around, hence the probable origin of the addition: 'Bristol fashion'. These problems were solved with the construction of a floating harbour which opened in 1809.

In the classic 1964 film version of *Mary Poppins*, Bert the lovable chimney sweep (played by Dick Van Dyke), delivers the following line in one of the worst Cockney accents ever to appear on celluloid:

> *Now this imposin' edifice what first meets the eye, is the 'ome of Admiral Boom, late of His Majesty's Navy. Likes his house shipshape he does. Shipshape and Bristol fashion at all times!*

With that in mind, perhaps it is best to leave the last word on this subject to a more reliable source. Admiral William Smyth defined the phrase in his *Sailor's Word Book:*

> *Said when Bristol was in its palmy commercial days … and its shipping was all in proper good order.*

To the bitter end

Kaiser Is Quoted as Determined Now to Go Through to the Bitter End.
   The New York Times, 16 February 1917

The phrase 'to the bitter end' is often used when referring to the eventual completion of a particularly long, arduous and troublesome task. For example, if one were to watch the whole of a singularly woeful and dreadfully long film until the credits finally start to roll (staying with the nautical theme *Titanic* springs to mind), then (apart from having one's sanity questioned) one could state they stuck with it 'to the bitter end'.

The term has nothing to do with anything tasting bitter. On a sailing ship it was vital that important cables, particularly those attached to anchors, did not run out and disappear overboard. Therefore the inboard ends of such cables were secured to a wooden post on the deck of a ship, which was known as a 'bitt'. Hence when a cable was let out to its maximum length it was said to be at the 'bitter end'; there was no more.

Copper bottomed

Rest assured, to be 'copper bottomed' has nothing to do with one's posterior. In modern usage, the term tends to be used to describe something, usually a business transaction or investment, that is secure or infallible (unsurprisingly, it is a staple headline on anything to do with the copper market!).

Building ships with wooden hulls created a major headache for ship designers; wooden hulls provided a home for *Teredo navalis,* the shipworm. These creatures are not technically worms, but a branch of the clam family found in tropical seas, and are often nicknamed 'termites of the sea'. *Teredo navalis* would bore into a ship's hull, causing extensive damage to the planking. Moreover, ships' bottoms often accumulated all sorts of other uninvited guests such as weeds and barnacles. All this weakened the strength of the hull and, with the extra drag, slowed the ship down. They had to be cleaned off at regular intervals in a dockyard or by careening, the process of beaching a ship so that one side of the hull was exposed and hence could be worked upon.

Many devices were used to address these problems: replaceable wooden planking, lead sheathing (which reacted with the iron bolts used in construction causing more damage) and graving – the process of applying various mixtures of tar, pitch, brimstone, rosin and train oil. None provided a suitable solution.

The use of copper was first suggested in Britain in 1708 but not acted upon (due to the high cost) until 1761 when the Admiralty ordered the Royal Navy's 32-gun frigate HMS *Alarm* to have her bottom covered with thin copper sheets. A mixture of hair, yarn and brown paper was first applied to the hull, and then the copper sheathing. Initial results were promising; copper reacts quickly with sea water to produce a thin, protective surface film. This film, of predominantly cuprous oxide, continues to mature over the next three-or-so months. Its protective value is enhanced by using copper alloyed with nickel or iron. This film provided a superb deterrent to weeds and *Teredo navalis*. However, the Admiralty discovered that, like the earlier experiments with lead, the copper sheathing also reacted with iron bolts used in the hull causing structural damage. A temporary return to lead sheathing was found to cause even more problems. In 1769 the Admiralty got to grips with the problem by building a ship with copper alloy bolts instead of the iron bolts traditionally used in hull construction. The American War of Independence (1775–83) at first got in the way of plans for the widespread adoption of coppering in the Royal Navy, but eventually turned out to be the catalyst. Britain was faced with the combined fleets of France, Spain and the Dutch Republic and needed every single ship to be at sea. In 1779 all ships up to 44 guns were to be coppered and this was shortly changed to the monumental decision to copper the entire fleet. Some issues remained with the copper alloy bolts until zinc was added; the Admiralty acted to use the new bolts across the entire fleet, finally solving the corrosion problem.

It was not just the Royal Navy that benefitted from copper-bottomed ships; the *Naval Chronicle* of 1799 reported the capture of a French privateer by HMS *Pomone*, Captain Reynolds, who tells the story:

> *We fortunately fell in with the Argus, and after a long chace [sic] of 180 miles running at 12 knots an hour, took her close up under Cape Finisterre. She is a beautiful ship, not six months off the stocks, carrying 18 brass nine pounders ... 130 men; is copper-bottomed, and a remarkable swift sailer.*

There'll be the Devil to pay

This is a common phrase used today to express rather unpleasant, perhaps even violent, consequences arising from an action or actions. The naval writer C. Northcote Parkinson used the phrase for the lead title of his 'Richard Delancey' series of novels, published in 1973, as *The Devil to Pay.*

In naval slang the phrase can allude to an unexpected situation, a state of unpreparedness or, according to Admiral Smyth, 'service expected, and no one ready to perform it'. The two phrases actually used are: **'the Devil to pay and only half a bucket of pitch'**, or sometimes **'the Devil to pay and no pitch hot'**.

This leaves us with the question: what is a devil, and why would sailors be paying him? The answer lies in the decks of wooden ships. In between each plank was a seam that had to be made watertight, this was done by forcing oakum into the seams and sealing it with hot pitch, a process called 'caulking', or in naval slang: **'paying'**. Oakum was old, frayed or unpicked rope and 'paying' was often a common punishment task for miscreants on board ship. The outermost seam,

where the deck met the hull, was notoriously difficult to caulk as it allowed little room for the sailor to use the caulking irons and mallet necessary to force the caulking in, hence it was nicknamed 'the devil'.

Some sources suggest another explanation pre-dating the naval phrase and originating from an agreement made to pay the Devil for some favour, i.e. selling one's soul for some kind of material gain during one's lifetime. As to why the Irish singer/songwriter Van Morrison chose this title for his 2006 album *Pay the Devil*, which consisted mainly of cover versions, one can only guess. Perhaps he was thinking of another naval phrase: '**money for old rope**'.

Between the devil and the deep blue sea

Continuing on the subject of the Devil, let's look at this lovely phrase. To recap, in a sailing warship the devil was the outermost seam between the planks of the deck and the hull. While a sailor was working on this seam, perhaps even hanging over the edge of the ship in a caulking seat, he was, literally, between the devil and the deep blue sea, a very precarious position to be in. The phrase has moved ashore and is used to describe someone who is faced with choosing between two unpleasant outcomes.

This was succinctly illustrated in 1932 when Ted Koehler penned the lyrics for a jazz song called 'Between the Devil and the Deep Blue Sea'. Originally recorded by the remarkable Cab Calloway, the song has remained a firm favourite with performing artists, including Ella Fitzgerald, Frank Sinatra and George Harrison. The lyrics describe the dilemma facing a spurned lover:

> *I don't want you*
> *But I hate to lose you*
> *You got me in between the devil and the*
> *deep blue sea*
>
> *I forgive you*
> *'Cause I can't forget you*
> *You've got me in between the devil and the*
> *deep blue sea*
>
> *I want to cross you off my list*
> *But when you come knocking at my door*
> *Fate seems to give my heart a twist*
> *And I come running back for more*
>
> *I should hate you*
> *But I guess I love you*
> *You've got me in between the devil and the*
> *deep blue sea*

Money for old rope

'Old rope' was just that, rope that had been used on the ship but had been replaced by new rope. Rope was often made from hemp imported from the Baltic States and had a multitude of uses on board ship, from rigging to anchor cables. The safety of the ship depended on good quality rope and any that was damaged or became worn was unsafe and had to be replaced. Moreover, although standing rigging (those ropes that supported the masts and did not move) could be waterproofed with tar, running rigging (used to control the yards and sails) could not be coated and had to be replaced on a regular basis. Nelson's flagship at Trafalgar, the 100-gun ship of the line HMS *Victory*, needed about 26 miles (42km) of rope just for her rigging! When all the other uses of rope on board ship are taken into account we can come to the conclusion that during the age of sail there must have been miles and miles of old rope knocking about.

One use for old rope was as oakum, but, as it also had many uses ashore, the crafty sailor could make some quick and easy money by selling it when in port. For example, from the seventeenth century onwards, bookbinders would pulp rope to make millboard, a strong substance used to make the boards for book covers. So 'money for old rope' is getting something for nothing, a phrase applicable today as people sell their unwanted stuff at yard, garage and car-boot sales, at flea markets and on Internet auctions.

Learn the ropes/Know the ropes

How many of us have started a new job and been told, 'You will be fine once you learn the ropes'? This phrase is commonly used to refer to the process of learning the skills and acquiring the experience necessary to perform a task.

Former United States Secretary of Defense Donald Rumsfeld decided to use this analogy when passing on some useful nuggets of wisdom:

> *Visit with your predecessors from previous Administrations. They know the ropes and can help you see around some corners. Try to make original mistakes, rather than needlessly repeating theirs.*

On a sailing warship it was important that everyone knew what they had to do at any particular moment: day or night, in calm weather or a howling gale, sailors' lives depended on speed and accuracy. Sailing warships were very complicated; they had miles of ropes and cordage for a number of different uses. Ropes were used to hoist sails, adjust yards and support the masts. The fairly standard layouts of the different types of sailing rig did allow this knowledge to be transferable to some extent, which was fine for experienced seamen. For the raw youngsters the hundreds of individual pieces, each with a distinct name, added up to a mind-boggling arrangement to get to grips with. Once the sailor had accumulated all this knowledge, it could be stated he knew the ropes. In fact this phrase was even used on sailors discharge certificates as a record of their competency.

Figurehead

In modern parlance the term 'figurehead' is regularly used as a metaphor to describe someone who is at the head of an organisation but in reality plays a small role, or no role at all, in decision making and therefore exercises very little power. Alternatively, it can describe a person who is employed purely so that an organisation can make use of their reputation and contacts. Again, they play a negligible role in the real decision making. The term is also applied in politics to presidents in parliamentary democracies and constitutional monarchs. For example, the role of the current Emperor of Japan, Akihito, is purely ceremonial; he plays no role in the government of his nation.

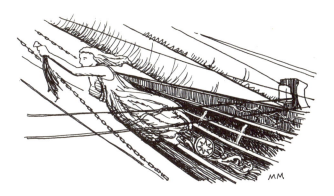

A figurehead, therefore, can be described as 'ornamental' and this is precisely what the nautical phrase means. A figurehead was a carved decoration adorning the bow of a ship which sailors (a deeply superstitious breed) often believed would have some supernatural ability to bring the ship luck. Subjects for the figurehead were chosen to reflect the name of the ship or, sometimes in merchant shipping, the wishes of the owner. The figurehead usually took either animal or human form in one of two styles, full-length or bust. A ship's figurehead was an important distinguishing feature and Lloyd's Register of Shipping would provide details of the figurehead in their description of a vessel. Moreover, the figurehead provided a unique mode of identification at sea for the usually illiterate sailors tasked with keeping a lookout.

The practice of adorning the bows of a ship stretches back in time. The Phoenicians and Greeks painted eyes on the prow of their galleys ensuring that the ship could see her way across the sea. The Carthaginians and Romans built upon this practice, installing carvings of gods on their ships to inspire sailors with confidence or to intimidate the enemy. The Vikings favoured sea serpents or dragon-like creatures to strike terror into the hearts of their foes. It seems as if the figurehead declined in popularity during the Middle Ages (due to the use of forecastles) only to reappear during the Renaissance. As states became more prosperous due to the global explosion in maritime trade, more money could be spent on naval force. Warships became bigger and more expensive and evolved into highly decorated symbols of state power. The ships of Phillip II in the Great Armada of 1588 naturally carried many religious figureheads of Catholic significance. These huge wooden decorated carvings of saints, the Virgin Mary and Jesus Christ, were eminently suitable for a campaign that based its chances of success on favour from God.

By Nelson's time the smaller, lighter and cheaper bust figure-head was favoured. HMS *Implacable* (the ex-French *Dugay Trouin*, captured in November

1805 after escaping the carnage of Trafalgar) carried a figurehead of the gorgon Medusa. A faithful replica of the figurehead from Nelson's flagship, HMS *Victory* can be seen today at Portsmouth's Royal Naval Dockyard. The figurehead consists of two cupids. One wears a red sash and hence is a Seraphim representing the love of God, and one wears a blue sash and hence is a Cherubim representing wisdom. They hold the royal coat of arms, topped off with the royal crown. The original figurehead cost £50 and was fitted sometime between 1801 and 1803; at Trafalgar the Cherubim lost a leg and the Seraphim an arm.

After the Napoleonic Wars the famous clipper ships tended to mount small, light full-length figures. Perhaps, the most famous was the tea clipper *Cutty Sark*'s 'Nannie the witch', inspired by Robert Burns' poem *Tam O'Shanter*. In true superstitious fashion, apprentices on board the *Cutty Sark* would make a horse's tail from old rope for 'Nannie' to hold in her outstretched arm. The original 'Nannie' is kept in the Cutty Sark Museum's collection and was therefore undamaged by the fire that swept through the preserved ship at Greenwich in May 2007.

The use of figureheads declined as iron and steel replaced wood as the primary shipbuilding material, instead the unique emblem of the ship became the ship's badge.

Batten down the hatches

This phrase has found widespread use ashore when trouble looms and preparations need to be made. Let's imagine you are at sea, there is a storm on the horizon, it looks like a bad one, what do you do? You 'batten down the hatches'. Openings in the deck were called hatchways and their covering was 'the hatch'. These were closed tight and covered using a sheet of canvas secured by a thin piece of wood (known as 'the batten') to prevent the ingress of water during a storm. Straightened hoops from casks could also be used as battens to secure the tarpaulin.

So, to 'batten down the hatches' is to prepare for a storm by making oneself secure, whether that be physically or metaphorically. On board HMS *Lord Nelson* in 1909 Midshipman Douglas King-Harman declared: 'Freezing hard, a strong easterly gale, the seas running very high … Of course we batten down all the hatches.' Given the origin of the phrase, it is no surprise the term is a favourite of weather forecasters warning of bad weather: 'Batten down hatches as gales sweep in' advised the *New Zealand Herald* on 28 April 2008. It is also a stock phrase in reports from the field of industry and commerce when unfavourable market conditions are predicted.

Skyscraper

The term 'skyscraper' was first used during the nineteenth century and was generally applied to anything taller than normal: a person, horse, or rider of the particularly tall Penny-farthing bicycle. Today it inevitably conjures up images of tall buildings; the Empire State Building, Canary Wharf Tower, or the current tallest building in the world, Taipei 101. It is difficult to state precisely when a building becomes a skyscraper; it is largely dependant on context. An unofficial guide is a minimum height of 150 metres or 500 feet. Initially the skyscraper was a distinctly American phenomenon. Towards the end of the nineteenth century the high cost of prime building land, particularly in the cities of Chicago and New York, led developers to look up to the skies. The resultant skyscraper craze of the 1920s and 1930s gripped Americans as New York took the title 'home of the skyscraper' with two monumental art deco buildings; the 1930 Chrysler Building and the 1931 Empire State Building. The skyscraper became an iconic image when used as the setting for the climactic scene of the 1933 blockbuster *King Kong.* The skyscraper remains a symbol of national power and prestige, even after the World Trade Center attacks of 9/11; Russia, China, Dubai and the USA are all currently building more of these concrete behemoths.

Of course, there is a nautical connection. These buildings were christened 'skyscrapers' after the name of a sail on a ship. The 'skyscraper sail' was the highest sail that could be set on a ship. Triangular in shape, it was positioned at the very top of the masts and was used only in light winds to get maximum propulsion. Viewed from deck it would seem that this high sail would almost be touching the sky.

When HMS *Eurydice* hove into view from the Isle of Wight in 1878, according to Bonchurch Coastguard Station she was 'moving fast under plain sail, studding sails on fore and main, bonnets and skyscrapers'; which was a big problem. Struck by a sudden squall, beset with blizzard-like winds and ice, it was impossible to take in the sails in time. Compounded by the fact *Eurydice* had her gunports open she was easily thrown over by the wind and sank taking all but two of her 366 crew to a watery grave. A short poem by Gerard Manley Hopkins summed up the dangers of setting such sails in bad weather:

Too proud, too proud, what a press she bore!
Royal, and all her royals wore.
Sharp with her, shorten sail!
Too late; lost; gone with the gale.

2

TAKEN ABACK

In the age of sail it seems logical that the process of moving a ship from A to B was called sailing. This term continues in usage today to describe a moving ship; modern warships do not carry sailing rigs but, despite this major consideration, when moving they are still described as sailing.

There are several ways to move a ship. Early seafarers quickly learned to harness the wind, though the unpredictability of the elements caused them to implement a back-up plan: oar power. The oar-powered galley was the mainstay of Mediterranean navies for centuries until the fully developed sailing rig appeared on the scene in the Middle Ages. It is from the classic age of the sailing warship, approximately 1600–1850, that the overwhelming majority of naval slang terms originate. Many relate to the actions of the elements upon the ship, whether that is the effect of the wind upon sails, or the position of the ship in relation to the sea. An experienced sailor would spend an enormous amount of his working time aloft in the rigging working the sails of a ship. The very word sailor is derived from one of the main components: sails.

A sailing warship was perhaps the most complicated piece of technology constructed until the industrial revolution of the early nineteenth century. Sailing itself was a complicated business requiring detailed knowledge of the winds, tides, submerged reefs, mathematical principles and the mastery of a range of other skills. It is not the intention to describe the complex principles of sailing here, but those interested will find plenty of literature on the subject. For much of history such sailing knowledge could only be acquired practically, i.e. by being at sea and working a ship and such experiences provided some useful additions to the sailor's vocabulary.

There are several types of sailing rig, though the two main ones used in warships were the square rig and the fore-and-aft rig. For people who have enjoyed movies such as *Master and Commander: The Far Side of the World* or the *Hornblower* series on television, or even visited HMS *Victory*, it is the square-rigged vessel that will be the most familiar. Such ships carry their main sails on yards, both of which are aligned perpendicular to the hull. The sails themselves are called square sails, even though they are not quite square. The yards, in turn, are attached to masts, the number of which varies: generally a sloop has only one, a brig two and larger warships three. Fore- and-aft rigged vessels differ as they carry their sails aligned along the line of the hull centre, in other words they follow the line of the keel which runs along the bottom of the ship. Again, the number of masts helps to define the type of ship: one mast for sloops and cutters, two for brigs and two or more for schooners. As you will notice, some types of ship can be either square- or fore- and aft-rigged. Moreover, just to confuse matters, a square-rigged vessel will set some sails in a fore-and-aft alignment.

Sailing rigs can be configured in a number of different ways. They were designed to combine the propulsion needed to move the hull forward in the water, all the time keeping the hull pointing in the right direction, yet minimising the risk of accidentally turning too much into the wind and the consequent risk of capsizing. This arrangement was called the 'sail plan' and usually comprised three basic layouts:

Light Air – large, lightweight sails designed for use in light winds.
Working – slightly heavier sails, with the layout designed to be changed to another plan at short notice.
Storm – sturdy and small sails for use in inclement weather to keep the ship stable and manageable.

With the ship suitably rigged for a voyage the next thing to do was plot the route. For many centuries navigation was a combination of skill, informed guess work and a fair amount of luck. Navigation is the process of deducing one's position relative to the surrounding world, thereby allowing a safe course to be set to the desired destination. The word itself comes from the Latin for ship, *navis*, and the action of moving, *agere*. During the age of sail a firm grasp of navigational skill was essential for any naval officer. As soon as he entered the navy, the lowly midshipman was expected to learn the basics. Surveying of marine passages and the production of sea charts was a rather hit-and-miss affair with little standardisation. Often, individuals would commission or purchase sea charts on their own initiative in advance of sailing. Recognising the failing of this system, the Admiralty founded the Royal Navy Hydrographic Office in 1795, with the first Admiralty-produced chart appearing in 1800. Such charts projected the spherical nature of the Earth onto a flat chart; a process known as Mercator's projection. The next vital piece of the navigator's kit was a compass. The modern-day compass probably originated in eleventh-century China and spread through the Mediterranean and from there to Western Europe. Other developments allowed the navigator to make accurate calculations. The sextant provided measurement of the height of celestial objects from the horizon at any given time; when used on board ship to take the noon reading it provided data to work out the ship's latitude. Finding one's longitude position was a more complicated matter, and not satisfactorily solved until the arrival of John Harrison's marine chronometer in the mid-eighteenth century.

The ship's speed was measured with a log or lead line. This was simply a knotted piece of rope which was thrown overboard. The number of knots that went out in a set period of time gave the speed in knots. This allowed the navigator to use a process called dead reckoning, i.e. the continual plotting of the course of a ship. With the ship's speed, heading and the time known, her estimated position could be projected onto a chart.

In harbours, anchorages, ports and off coastlines a person with local knowledge of the area would be engaged to provide advice or even to navigate the ship. This person would guide the ship through a safe course, and was known as a pilot.

In the nineteenth century sail gave way to steam power from coal-fired boilers, which in turn gave way to oil and finally to nuclear power. Yet, despite these developments, we still use many terms relating to the methods of sailing a wooden warship.

Taken aback

And with a bow Dete quickly left the room and ran downstairs. Fraulein Rottenmeier stood for a moment taken aback and then ran after Dete.
Heidi by Johanna Spyri

In 2006 when Pakistan's President General Pervez Musharraf made claims that the United States had threatened to bomb Pakistan 'to the Stone Age' if it failed to cooperate in the aftermath of 9/11, President George Bush declared he was 'taken aback by the harshness of the words' (*Washington Post*, 23 September 2006). Commentators are still unsure what definition President Bush was using, as 'to be taken aback' is to be surprised by a turn or events or a situation, perhaps even to a state of inaction or confusion.

The term relates to a sailing phenomenon where the wind blows against the wrong side of the sails, thereby pushing them back onto the masts, spars and rigging. In strong winds this was a very dangerous situation and could damage the sailing rig. It could be caused by a ship sailing too close to the wind and being caught by a sudden change in wind direction. Moreover, alongside the potential for material damage, a ship could be left vulnerable by the sudden loss of momentum. Such is the fate of the Turkish ship *Torgud* towards the end of Patrick O'Brian's book *Ionian Mission*. HMS *Surprise*, captained by the heroic Jack Aubrey, is faced with fighting two Turkish ships *Torgud* and *Kitabi*. At one point in the battle *Surprise* is faced by the more heavily manned *Torgud*, and to prevent being boarded, Aubrey turns *Surprise* into the wind. As a consequence of trying to follow the manoeuvre, *Torgud* is 'taken aback' and falls behind the *Surprise* allowing Aubrey to successfully deal with each ship in turn, rather than as a combined force.

On occasion, however, being 'taken aback' could be used to purposely halt the movement of a ship. In battle this tactic could bring a ship to a sudden halt, allowing an enemy ship to shoot ahead or one's own ship to fall away from an opponent. This was precisely what happened in the combat between the 32-gun frigate HMS *Thames* and the French ship *Uranie*, 40-guns. William James, in his *Naval History of Great Britain*, describes what happened:

> *An action now commenced … Uranie, getting under the stern of the* Thames, *gave her two or three raking broadsides, and then attempted to board … but, on receiving through her bows a well-directed fire from six or seven of the* Thames's *maindeck guns, double-shotted, the* Uranie *threw all her sails aback, and hauled off to the southward. The British crew, on seeing this, gave three hearty cheers …*

Take the wind out of his/her sails

This phrase is commonly used to describe the practice of gaining an advantage over someone by slowing or stopping their actions or words. After seeing his England team slump to a record sixth defeat (England 20:New Zealand 41) on the bounce in November 2006, England Rugby head coach Andy Robinson referred to a controversial decision to not give a try early in the game, lamenting, 'When it was disallowed it took the wind out of our sails'. Perhaps trying a little too hard to shoehorn this phrase into a piece about outbreaks of food poisoning on cruise ships in 2003 the *Washington Diplomat* ran an article with the catchy title 'Norwalk Virus May Take Wind Out of Sails on Cruise Ship Vacations'.

Naturally, the term is derived from a sneaky sailing manoeuvre designed to slow down or even stop an opponent's ship by interposing one's own ship between the opponent and the weather gauge (the wind direction), thereby denying the opponent sufficient wind to propel their ship. Gaining such an advantage over an opponent could be a telling factor in naval battle and it is still a particularly favoured tactic in modern sailing and yachting contests. In the movie *Master and Commander: The Far Side of the World*, Captain Jack Aubrey intentionally takes the wind out of his own sails as a *ruse de guerre*:

> '... we must bring them right up beside us before we spring this trap. That will test our nerve, and discipline will count just as much as courage. The **Acheron** is a tough nut to crack ... more than twice our guns, more than twice our numbers, and they will sell their lives dearly. Topmen, your handling of the sheets to be lubberly and un-navy like. Until the signal calls, you're to spill the wind from our sails, this will bring us almost to a complete stop.'

Backing and filling

This term is habitually used by the finance and business communities to describe the many small rises and falls in market stock prices. The prices fluctuate regularly but without any major effect on the overall value of the actual commodity. An example from *The New York Times* of 29 June 1922 will suffice: 'After backing and filling during the morning, cotton advanced half a cent from low figures yesterday, closing 23 to 36 points up.' It can also describe someone who fluctuates in their decision-making or their arguments.

Backing and filling a ship's sails was a method of making very small changes in position in a confined space, such as a harbour or anchorage, or to try to maintain a general position either on, against, or with the tide. A ship could change her sail arrangements (trimming sails) to catch the wind, thereby moving her forward, or could back them, in effect pushing them back again the masts (see **taken aback**) and moving the ship backwards. In doing so the ship moves backwards and forwards.

A person can also perform the same manoeuvre; here an anonymous author described the motions of a fictional drunken reveller:

> ... he wound up his wondrous performance by reeling gracefully up to the youthful Countess of Livorno, with the 'rolling motion,' and 'backing and filling' twice around her, each time imprinting a kiss on her cherry-coloured lips.
> 'Que Diablo de hombre!' cried the Spanish ambassador.
> 'C'est un veritable bête!' said the marquis.
> 'C'est un ange!' sighed his wife.
>
> 'Life of a Midshipman' in *The Knickerbocker: Or, New York Monthly Magazine*, 1858

Sailing close to the wind

A sailing ship needs wind to sail and when a ship wants to go in the same direction as the wind, referred to as 'running', then all is fine. However, when a sailor wants to sail in a different direction things can get a bit tricky, especially when a ship needs to go against the direction of the wind. When a ship does sail into the wind the sails can be set to catch the wind and that force combined with the shape of the hull will allow the ship to make some forward progress. If a ship tries to sail too far into the wind it will lose propulsion. Staying on the correct side of this point is known as 'sailing close to the wind'.

Ashore, the phrase has become synonymous with taking a risk or pushing one's luck to the limit without pushing it too far. For example, on 15 May 2008 Reuters observed: 'Prime Minister Gordon Brown insisted on Thursday he would not break the fiscal rules he has followed since 1997, but his backing for a package of tax cuts this week leaves him sailing very close to the wind'.

It is no surprise that yachtsman Pete Goss chose the phrase 'Close to the Wind' for his autobiography. While competing in the 1996 Vendée Globe solo round-the-world yacht race, Goss heroically risked his ship and his life to turn back into tremendous winds and rescue capsized French competitor Raphaël Dinelli.

High and dry

To be left 'high and dry' is to be stuck in a rather difficult situation and unable to find a way out. For instance, property investors could be left 'high and dry' if the bottom fell out of the housing market. The term 'high and dry' refers to the state of a ship when out of the water. This could be for two reasons. First, if a ship had the misfortune to run aground those parts normally below the waterline would be exposed when the tide receded. The ship, now out of the water, could obviously not move and hence would be 'high and dry'. The second way that a ship could be 'high and dry' was if she were taken into a dockyard and left on the stocks, either for repair or in a dry dock. This was known as being in 'ordinary', a sort of mothballing for ships that were not in active service. During the age of sail governments often tried to save money by laying ships up in ordinary and paying off their crews until the next conflict.

One of the most famous ships to be left 'high and dry' was the 80-gun third rate ship of the line HMS *Foudroyant*, a former flagship of Lord Nelson's. In 1897 when *Foudroyant* was being used as a boy's training ship

she was driven onto the sand at Blackpool in a howling gale. Wrecked beyond repair, entrepreneurs cashed in by taking striking photographs of her lying in the shadow of Blackpool tower while others salvaged her timbers to make furniture, a sad end for a long-serving veteran of the wars against France.

Plain sailing

The fabled North-West Passage, the sea route through the Arctic, around the top of North America, was first navigated by Roald Amundsen in 1903–06, but the thick Arctic ice prevented extensive commercial use. Recent global warming is causing shrinkage in the ice as media sources informed the world in 2007:

North-West Passage is now plain sailing
  The Guardian, 28 August 2007
Plain sailing on the Northwest Passage
  BBC News, 19 September 2007

Both *The Guardian* and the BBC indicate that sailing through the once dangerous North-West Passage is now a relatively straightforward task.

'Plain sailing' should, technically, be 'plane sailing'. 'Plane sailing' was the process of navigating from the assumption that the earth was flat, hence the ship was actually positioned on a *planum* (Latin for flat surface). With no confusing calculations to take into account lines of latitude (horizontal lines running parallel to the equator) and longitude (curved meridians running north to south with Greenwich as the prime meridian) 'plane sailing' was a relatively easy method of navigating. To calculate a course, sailors would plot a plane sailing triangle by drawing a meridian down through the point of departure, a line of latitude through the point of destination then join up the two points to plot the course – thereby forming a triangle. The term 'plain' was commonly used instead of 'plane' due to the simplicity of the method. Ashore the term 'plain sailing' stuck and became a way to describe anything that was relatively easy, straightforward or without undue complications. According to Admiral Smyth's *Sailor's Word Book*:

> *Plane-sailing is so simple that it is colloquially used to express anything so easy that it is impossible to make a mistake.*

Sail under false colours

It has been a long maritime tradition that ships fly their national colours from the stern as it allows for easy identification. But it also provided the perfect means to implement a classic nautical ruse. By flying 'false colours' it was possible to lure an unsuspecting enemy into a trap or to get close with one's own ship by misrepresenting one's intentions. It is a trick beloved of naval fiction writers, but it was a widespread *ruse de guerre*, often favoured by cruisers (single ships deployed to prey on the trade of the enemy), privateers and, of course, fearsome pirates. It was an acceptable practice, as long as the false colours were hauled down and replaced by the real colours prior to opening fire. During both World Wars the Royal Navy and the US Navy used 'Q' ships; special merchant ships kitted out with hidden weaponry. They were used to lure unsuspecting German and Japanese submarines into surfacing to attack them, because a submarine on the surface is easier to sink than one beneath the waves.

The term has crept ashore to be applied in a number of ways. Georgette Heyer, in her 1963 regency pot-boiler *False Colours* details the story of a young man who impersonates his twin brother. The term can be also used in a more derogatory way to describe people who don't reveal their true intentions, who are, perhaps, hiding some dark and fiendish activity or plan. It is no surprise then that Richard Woodman chose *Under False Colours* as the title for the tenth instalment of his Nathaniel Drinkwater series of naval fiction books. The hero Drinkwater, by now a Captain in the Royal Navy, is sent on a secret mission, going undercover as a merchant mariner to sow discord between France and Russia.

Perhaps the most famous exploit using the 'false colours' ruse was implemented by Lord Thomas Cochrane, the most daring captain of the Napoleonic Wars. In May 1801 Cochrane was in command of HMS *Speedy*, a 14-gun brig manned by a crew of 54 when he came upon the Spanish *xebec* (frigate), *El Gamo*. Cochrane initially eyed up his opponent by flying Danish colours, even stationing an officer in Danish uniform on deck. Cochrane realised he was outnumbered and outgunned: the *Gamo* carried 32 guns and a crew of 319 men. Cochrane sailed away, but came upon the *Gamo* again a few days later. This time, with the Spaniard unaware of his real intentions, Cochrane got *Speedy* so close that the *Gamo* could not depress her guns to fire on Cochrane's ship. At this point he signalled the attack and began a 45-minute cannonade of the superior foe. Metal tore through wood and flesh on the Spanish ship until Cochrane made the signal to board and led forty valiant souls to attack five times their number in brutal hand-to-hand combat. As the fight hung in the balance, Cochrane nonchalantly and very loudly ordered over the side for another fifty men to board the *Gamo* – there were, in fact, only three left on his ship! At this the fight went out of the Spaniards and Cochrane completed one of the most remarkable acts of derring-do in the annals of naval history – and all thanks to 'sailing under false colours'.

Hard to fathom/To sound something out

A fathom is an old nautical unit of measurement used for distances and depths. The Admiralty defined the fathom as 6.08ft; precisely one thousandth of a nautical mile which measured 6080ft. Sailors would often round the fathom down to a simple 6ft, making calculations a lot easier. The

word itself comes from the old Anglo-Saxon word *fæðm*, to embrace, which referred to the distance along the outstretched arms of a person when about to embrace. This distance then became a standard unit of measurement.

When sailors wanted to find out how deep the water was they would use a lead (or sounding) line marked off into fathoms to find the bottom. This was known as sounding out or taking soundings (hence the phrase, 'to sound someone out', means to work out what their intentions are). If the sailor found the bottom, he had **got to the bottom of things**, but if he had difficulty finding the exact depth, it was, literally, hard to fathom. Ashore the phrase is used when someone or something is hard to understand. Therefore 'to **fathom out**' a problem is to find a solution.

Give them a wide berth

Today, ships are usually moored to a dockside or quay, i.e. securely 'berthed'. In the age of sail, however, ships often berthed in harbours using only their anchors to keep them in place. According to Smyth, a good place to berth was 'in good anchoring ground, well sheltered from the wind and sea, and at a proper distance from the shore and other vessels'. Sailing ships riding at anchor would move with the tide and the wind, hence when they were berthed they had to leave enough sea room to take this movement into account. So, another ship passing a ship at anchor would give them a 'wide berth' to ensure that there was no risk of an accidental collision. In modern-day usage, the meaning has been refined to include the actual avoidance of something, rather than just passing at a safe distance.

In 'Letter 10' of his 1831 publication *Letters on Demonology and Witchcraft*, Sir Walter Scott illustrates the use of the phrase in describing the perilous situation facing a farmer:

> *He was pondering with some anxiety upon the dangers of travelling alone on a solitary road which passed the corner of a churchyard, now near at hand, when he saw before him in the moonlight a pale female form standing upon the very wall which surrounded the cemetery. The road was very narrow, with no opportunity of giving the apparent phantom what seamen call a wide berth.*

On occasion the usual convention of avoiding anchored ships has been completely ignored in order to gain an advantage in naval battle. This is best illustrated at the Battle of Aboukir Bay (Battle of the Nile) of 1 August 1798. The French Admiral Brueys had seemingly taken up a secure defensive position, anchoring his ships in a line close by the shore, but leaving enough room for them to swing safely if the wind changed. On board his flagship, the 74-gun HMS *Vanguard*, Admiral Lord Horatio Nelson spotted this, as his Flag Captain Sir Edward Berry later recounted:

> *The position of the Enemy presented the most formidable obstacles; but the Admiral viewed these with the eye of a Seaman determined on attack; and it instantly struck his eager and penetrating mind, that where there was room for an Enemy's Ship to swing, there was room for one of ours to anchor. No further Signal was necessary than those which had already been made. The Admiral's designs were as fully known to his whole Squadron, as was his determination to conquer, or perish in the attempt.*

In fact it was Captain Thomas Foley of the *Goliath*, leading the British attack that observed at first hand the gap between the French ships and the shore.

He sailed *Goliath* round the head of the French fleet before anchoring on the landward side and engaging the enemy ships. She was followed by four more British ships, and, as the rest of the fleet took up a position on the seaward side, the lead French ships were caught between two fires. Foley's initiative was the decisive action of the battle and the French fleet was crushed. At a single stroke, British dominance of the Mediterranean had been secured, and all because Foley had ignored the maritime convention of giving anchored ships 'a wide berth'.

On your beam ends

This interesting phrase has a couple of meanings. The most widespread definition is to be in a singularly difficult or tricky situation, with, perhaps, more than a hint of danger. Another possible use is highlighted in Smyth's *Sailor's Word Book* which mentions that it can also apply to someone in a prone position; while a third, though not really commonly used, is when describing a state of financial ruin.

In nautical terms if a ship is on her beam ends, then she is most certainly in a dangerous position. Ships' beams were the transverse pieces of timber that stretched across the shape of the hull and were attached to the side with timbers known as 'ships' knees'. Thus positioned, the beams provided the base for the deck structure and strength to the hull sides. If a ship heeled over so that her sides were almost touching the water, then she was said to be 'on her beam ends'; i.e. her beams would be almost vertical to the water. Finding herself in such a predicament, a ship was in great danger of completely going over and capsizing. Drastic times often called for drastic measures – the crew of a ship in such a position often had to jettison weight in order to right the ship, this might entail cutting away the masts and sending them over the sides, dumping cargo or even cannons.

Such a fate befell the warship USS *Yantic*, caught in a hurricane off the Eastern US Seaboard during May of 1889. Commander J. C. Rockwell told *The New York Times* what happened next:

> … *we were struck by a hurricane from the south … Everything had been made as snug as possible. But the force of the wind was terrific, and at the height of the storm, we were thrown on our beam ends. The sea, which was very high, climbed directly into the steam launch, which was on the lee side, and filled it with water. Orders were at once given to cut away the launch, but the loss of its weight still failed to right us. It was then found necessary*

to cut away the foremast and then went by the board, carrying with it the maintopmast and later the mizzentopmast.

This did the trick and the ship righted herself, much to Commander Rockwell's relief. She had been on her beam ends for around an hour. Even ships without a sailing rig can find themselves in this predicament. In 1915 the French pre-dreadnought battleship *Bouvet* struck a mine in the confined waters of the Dardanelles and started to list. One eyewitness records:

> *… she was on her beam ends … Then she was bottom up with her screws in the air & then nothing but a cloud of black smoke & great commotion in the water. It was all over in less than three minutes.*

Bouvet took over 600 men with her to the bottom.

Bearing up

When faced with an adverse situation or turn of events one is frequently asked by interested parties, 'how are you bearing up?'

This old sailing term originates from the instruction by the skipper to the helmsman to bring the ship closer to the wind, thereby 'bearing up' into the wind – 'bearing' being the course of a ship. Depending on the weather conditions, this could be an uncomfortable procedure. The term is aptly described in Nathaniel Bowditch's *New American Practical Navigator* of 1826:

> *The act of changing the course of a ship, in order to make her run before the wind … it is generally performed to arrive at some port under the lee, or to avoid some imminent danger occasioned by a violent storm, leak, or enemy in sight.*

Cut and run

> *Karen (Emma Thompson): 'Imagine your husband bought a gold necklace and come Christmas gave it to somebody else …'*
> *Harry (Alan Rickman): 'Oh, Karen …'*
> *Karen: 'Would you wait around to find out if it's just a necklace, or if it's sex and a necklace, or if worst of all it's a necklace and love? Would you stay, knowing life would always be a little bit worse? Or would you cut and run?'*
> Love Actually

'Cut and run' basically means to 'get the hell outta here!' It possibly derives from two actions that were necessary to get a sailing ship underway quickly. On a square-rigged ship riding at anchor, the sails could be furled and secured by tying them to the yards, in order to set the sails quickly the securing lines would be cut and the sails would fall into place and catch the wind. 'Run' is to run with the wind, i.e. to have it directly behind.

Another explanation comes from when an anchored ship wanted to make a quick escape from potential danger or enemy action; the anchor cable would literally be cut. The process of hauling in an anchor could be a lengthy process, requiring a raw muscle power, provided by landsmen, to turn the capstan. This was a large cylindrical device around which the anchor cable would be wound, effectively a giant winch. The capstan had protruding poles for the landsmen to push against, hence they would walk in a circle turning the capstan and hauling in the anchor. Tasks such as this were often accompanied by a suitable sea shanty, such as the reference 'heave-ho' and the 'up she rises' of the anchor in perhaps the most famous sea shanty of the all 'The Drunken Sailor':

> *What shall we do with a drunken sailor,*
> *What shall we do with a drunken sailor,*
> *What shall we do with a drunken sailor,*
> *Early in the morning?*
>
> *Heave-ho and up she rises,*
> *Heave-ho and up she rises,*
> *Heave-ho and up she rises,*
> *Early in the morning.*

Hauling in the anchor using the capstan would take time; so instead the ship would 'cut and run' thereby ensuring a quick get away.

Free and easy

> *Thursday's quiz night – it always has been. Thursday's quiz night; Wednesday's free and easy night. You can't go rearranging days.*
> Jerry St Clair, Compere, The Phoenix Club, *Phoenix Nights*

How can a nautical saying make the transition to a British TV comedy series based around a Bolton nite-spot? In *Phoenix Nights* Jerry St Clair's 'free and easy' night is a casual, relaxed evening of good old-fashioned variety entertainment – singing, magic tricks and, occasionally, the odd bit of martial arts.

Looking back to the nautical origins of the phrase, 'free' relates to a rope which is clear for running, i.e. it is not obstructed in any way. According to Smyth, a ship is '**going free**' when 'the bowlines are slacked and the sheets eased'. Therefore, the ropes and tackle which control the sails are in a nice and relaxed state, hence are 'free' and 'eased'. This is often the case when the wind is blowing from the stern.

Carried away

We all know the dangers of getting 'carried away' in a situation. It implies a loss of control of one's actions, of getting too excited and allowing that to impact on our judgement. Jérôme Kerviel, a junior French stock trader at the bank Société Générale, hit the headlines in 2007 after bringing the financial institution to its knees by betting around £3.7 billion on rapidly falling stocks. His explanation? He described himself as getting 'a little carried away'. In modern usage it is also used in a negative way as a warning after a success or achievement, for example 'now, don't get carried away'.

Afloat the term has a more precise meaning. Sailors would use the phrase to describe something aboard ship that had (often violently) broken, usually yards, masts or ropes. For example, 'A gust of wind, whilst we were off the Azores, carried away our top-masts and our sails, tearing the latter in shreds as if they had been sheets of paper...' James Johnstone recalled in his *Memoirs of the Rebellion in 1745 and 1746*.

All at sea

To be 'all at sea' is to be in a state of confusion or bewilderment; to be lost either emotionally, physically or mentally. It is derived from the position of a ship that has lost its bearings; it is literally, all at sea.

Award-winning pint-sized crooner Jamie Cullum included a track entitled 'All at Sea' on his platinum-selling 2003 album *Twentysomething*, which rather nicely sums up the feeling behind the phrase (though some might say he was ruminating on his lot as a supporter of Swindon Town Football Club):

> *All at sea*
> *I'm all at sea*
> *Where no-one can bother me*
> *I sleep by myself*
> *I drink on my own*
> *Don't speak to nobody*

Touch and go

When something is 'touch and go' it might or might not happen; it indicates a state of flux, of uncertainty as to the eventual conclusion of a situation. Taken to the extreme, it can be used to describe a perilous or risky situation. This is understandable when we look at the origins of the term. When a ship accidentally ran aground, but was lucky enough to shift off the bottom almost immediately (as could often happen in harbour or on submerged sandbanks or reefs) without any serious damage she had literally been in a 'touch and go' situation – touching but getting going again.

Some sources also point to another old nautical definition of the phrase referring to the activities of a ship heading into port for a brief amount of time before heading straight back out to sea and on to her eventual destination. Interestingly, it is also used in aviation slang to describe the practice taught to trainee pilots of making a landing approach, briefly touching the wheels on the runway, then taking off again, a remarkably similar action to a ship touching the bottom and going off on her course.

3

THE OGGIN

For much of history, a life spent at sea was a dangerous existence. In fact the sailor was more likely to suffer serious injury or die from accident and disease than enemy action. As Brian Lavery calculated in *Nelson's Navy*, during the French Revolutionary and Napoleonic Wars the Royal Navy lost about 6,500 men in action with enemy ships. Shipwreck and fire accounted for another 13,000 but the largest number, around 70–80,000, were lost due to disease and accidents. Even today, with modern ship designs, global satellite positioning and 24/7 weather reports the sailor is still exposed to the hazards of the sea. On 12 November 2007 one Georgian and four Russian ships went down in the Black Sea in bad weather. Moreover, accidents still happen: the Soviet submarine *K-19* suffered a nuclear-reactor coolant leak, a collision with USS *Gato* and a fire during her career, claiming the lives of nearly sixty of her crew – no wonder she was nicknamed 'The Widowmaker'.

For the sailor death could come in many forms, some from just going about his daily routine. A momentary lapse in concentration or a misplaced foot or hand could see a man fall from the rigging onto the deck below, usually resulting in fatal or very serious injuries. In stormy weather, when changes to the sails had to be done quickly, the danger was even more obvious. Masts and spars could be carried away by the wind and waves, sending men tumbling into the water or onto the deck. Caught in a storm in May 1798 HMS *Vanguard*'s Captain Edward Berry recounted: 'the main top-mast went over the side, with the top-sail yard full of men', but fortunately lost he only two men: 'one man fell overboard, and one fell on the booms, and was killed on the spot'. Those who did die on board ship were dealt with in the time-honoured tradition; their bodies were stitched up in their hammocks (with the final stitch put through the nose to make sure they were dead) and then committed to the deep, after which their personal belongings were sold to their shipmates.

In the twentieth century running into foul weather could still be deadly. Alfred Carpenter was on board the destroyer HMS *Caldwell*, an old US-built 'four stacker', on escort duty in the North Atlantic during the winter of 1942–3, when she ran into a hurricane. With the ship and her crew battered and bruised: 'the Chief Stoker could not be found. He never was … He had presumably been washed overboard. In the howling winds and commotion that prevailed, no cry for help would have been heard, nor could anything have been done if it had'.

Compounding such tragedy, before the twentieth century many sailors could not swim, so falling overboard at sea was most likely fatal. This was before the introduction of modern swimming strokes and officers were unwilling to teach the men to swim for fear of them absconding when near to shore. Sailors looked upon this stoically; if the ship went down in the middle of the ocean then swimming would only prolong the inevitable end. On occasion, a quick-thinking officer could slow the progress of the ship and lower a boat to pluck a man from the sea, although this did not always result in a positive outcome. Witness the fate of one of HMS *Victory*'s crew in September 1805: 'At 7.30 fell overboard Rob[er]t Chandler (S) Backed the Main Top Sail & sent a Boat to look for him but could not find him'. Even those who could swim were not always saved. In 1939 the submarine HMS *Triton* accidentally torpedoed another British submarine HMS *Oxley*. Finding three survivors in the water *Triton* rescued two, who turned out to be Lieutenant Commander Bowerman and Able Seaman Gukes. According to *Triton*'s commander, Lieutenant Commander H. P. de C. Steel, the other man 'was seen swimming strongly in the light of an Aldis [lamp] when he suddenly disappeared and was seen no more'.

Probably the most dangerous situation for a sailing warship was to be caught in a storm. With high winds and heavy swells ships could be blown towards the shore where the prospect of running aground and breaking up was a very real one indeed. In such instances the ship could be dashed against rocks with corpses of the crew, mangled by the sea, eventually washed ashore.

Sometimes such disasters could be caused by human error. In 1707 Rear Admiral Sir Cloudesley Shovell's squadron ran aground on the Scilly Isles. Several ships were wrecked and about 1,400 men, including Shovell himself, lost their lives due to navigational errors.

Two centuries later such incidents still occurred. HMS *Birkenhead*, an iron-hulled troopship carrying the 73rd Regiment of Foot and detachments from other regiments, ran into a submerged rock off Cape Town. With the ship clearly sinking, Lieutenant-Colonel Seton took control of the situation drawing the soldiers up on deck, allowing the women and children to take to the serviceable lifeboats first and thereby giving the world the first ever orderly 'women and children first' evacuation. As the ship broke up underneath them the soldiers still maintained their ranks on deck, Seton knew that if they panicked they would swamp the already full lifeboats, putting the women and children at risk. Of 643 people on board only 193 survived, the majority lost were either drowned or eaten by sharks. 'Remember the Birkenhead' became a stock phrase for Victorian stoicism, and the episode was celebrated in 1898 by Rudyard Kipling:

> *To take your chance in the thick of a rush, with firing all about,*
> *Is nothing so bad when you've cover to 'and, an' leave an' likin' to shout;*
> *But to stand an' be still to the Birken'ead drill*
> *is a damn tough bullet to chew,*
> *An' they done it, the Jollies – 'Er Majesty's Jollies –*
> *soldier an' sailor too!*
> *Their work was done when it 'and't begun; they was younger*
> *nor me an' you;*
> *Their choice it was plain between drownin' in 'eaps*
> *an' bein' mopped by the screw,*
> *So they stood an' was still to the Birken'ead drill, soldier an' sailor too!*

In some cases ships and their crews have just disappeared, never to be seen again. With the introduction of submarines in the twentieth century the phenomenon of ships simply vanishing at sea became more acute. In fact the first submarine ever to sink a warship, the Confederate *H. L. Hunley*, sank with all hands shortly after detonating her meagre payload which holed the USS *Housatonic* on 17 February 1864. One of the Royal Navy's greatest submarine commanders of the Second World War, Lieutenant-Commander Malcolm Wanklyn VC disappeared with his crew and his submarine HMS *Upholder* in April 1942.

Yet, just as the sea can take from the sailor it can also provide. Many a sailor, cast adrift or shipwrecked, has survived due to the bounty provided by marine life. Seabirds, turtles and their eggs, fish, seals, and even polar bears have all ended up on the dinner plate of the hungry sailor. Surrounded by the sea and its strange fauna, at the mercy of the winds, waves and rocks, with the ever-present possibility of an untimely death, it is no surprise that the sailor incorporated what he saw around him into his language.

Booby prize

The booby prize is a useless award given to a competitor who finishes last or has the worst performance in a competition or a game. It can also be awarded to honour an achievement of outstanding stupidity. The actual object that forms the prize is usually specifically selected to represent the ineptitude of

the winner and can become a subject of much mirth and hilarity. On the British cult TV game show *3-2-1*, presented by Ted Rogers, the booby prize was a real plastic bin (trash can). In professional sports teams the player with the worst performance in training is often awarded a booby prize. This can take many forms, a few noteworthy examples are wearing old and unwashed sweaty training gear, wearing a yellow bib emblazoned with the phrase 'I am shite' or driving a particularly embarrassing car to work, such as the three-wheeled Robin Reliant. Moreover, playing on the humiliation aspect of the booby prize, in popular parlance to make a 'boob' is to make a great fool of oneself in a particularly dumb way.

So what was a 'booby'? The first answer to spring to mind is that it relates to female breasts. It is fairly obvious why the UNISON-sponsored award made to organisations that are the least co-operative to mothers wishing to breastfeed is called the 'Booby Prize' (the inaugural winner in 2006 was McDonalds). Certainly some sources point to sailors calling mammary glands 'boobies' after a famous tropical seabird: the booby. These large birds, part of the *Pelecaniformes* family and related to the gannets, dive into the sea from a height to catch fish. They were also prone to perching on the yards of a ship or even landing on deck. This made it particularly easy for sailors to catch and eat them; hence ship's crews thought they were exceptionally stupid and which is the real origin of 'booby'.

One the most famous consumers of the booby bird was Captain William Bligh of 'Mutiny on the *Bounty*' fame. In April 1789 Bligh and eighteen of his crew were cast adrift in a 23ft open launch by Fletcher Christian and his fellow mutineers. Bligh, in a remarkable piece of navigation, made a 47-day voyage to Timor, a distance of 3,618 nautical miles. In his own account of the voyage, Bligh detailed what they lived on:

> *Tuesday, 26th [May] – Fresh breezes from the S.E., with fine weather. In the morning we caught another booby, so that Providence appeared to be relieving our wants in an extraordinary manner.*

And again on Thursday 11 June:

> *In the afternoon, we saw gannets, and many other birds, and at sunset we kept a very anxious look-out. In the evening we caught a booby, which I reserved for our dinner the next day.*

Taking things even further back to the fourteenth and fifteenth centuries when Spanish galleons ruled the waves, it is no surprise to learn that the Spanish slang term for fool, *bobo*, was applied to the strange seabirds which were foolish enough to allow the Spanish sailors to capture them with ease. The term then entered the English language as 'booby' and its consequent usage for stupidity or failure.

In the doldrums

> *All in a hot and copper sky,*
> *The bloody Sun, at noon,*
> *Right up above the mast did stand,*
> *No bigger than the Moon.*
>
> *Day after day, day after day,*
> *We stuck, nor breath nor motion;*
> *As idle as a painted ship*
> *Upon a painted ocean.*
>
> The Rime of the Ancient Mariner by Samuel Taylor Coleridge

What Coleridge was referring to in these famous stanzas from his epic poem was the phenomenon known across the globe as the 'doldrums'.

The doldrums are the equatorial regions of the Atlantic and Pacific Oceans – in technical speak they are the Intertropical Convergence Zone.

Here, low pressure is present and this causes either extended periods of calm wind conditions, or the complete opposite of squalls or even hurricane strength storms. Sailing ships in the area can lose their propulsion for days or weeks on end or be hit by horrendous weather. In *Following the Equator*, Mark Twain described it thus:

> *We entered the 'doldrums' last night – variable winds, bursts of rain, intervals of calm, with chopping seas and a wobbly and drunken motion to the ship – a condition of things findable in other regions sometimes, but present in the doldrums always.*

No one is sure if the term originated at sea and came ashore or the other way round. Some commentators point to a combination of 'dolorous' (sad) or *dol* (dull) and 'tantrums', referring to the nature of the weather conditions. Others suggest that 'doldrum' was a term applied to those who were 'dull or sluggish' – characteristics often displayed by those in low spirits. The term might then have gone afloat to refer to the area we now know as the doldrums. Ships' crews becalmed in the extreme heat of the doldrums were often afflicted by severe depression and quick tempers, a feeling expressed by David Gilmour in 'Lost for words', the penultimate track on Pink Floyd's *The Division Bell* album:

> *I was spending my time in the doldrums*
> *I was caught in a cauldron of hate*
> *I felt persecuted and paralysed*
> *I thought that everything else would just wait*

But perhaps our modern use of the term is best left to a master wordsmith; Hunter S. Thompson. According to close friends, Thompson found the elation of the Super Bowl final, which marks the end of the NFL season each January, was replaced by his cruel 'doldrums time' the following month. He shot himself on 20 February 2005.

In the offing

Next time you hear someone use this phrase, ask them, 'So, what *exactly* is an offing?' and see if they really know what they are talking about. It is most commonly used to describe something that might or will happen in the near future which has a particular presence or impact on the current situation. For example, with increasing global concerns about the proliferation of nuclear weapons, the UK newspaper *The Guardian* in May 2007 posed the question: 'Armageddon in the offing?'

It is no surprise that P. G. Wodehouse chose *Jeeves in the Offing* as the title for the ninth instalment in his popular series of books. While visiting his Aunt Dahlia our loveable, but hapless, hero Bertie Wooster is confronted by the usual eclectic mix of eccentric individuals including his ex-fiancée Bobbie Wickham, psychiatrist Sir Roderick Glossop, Aubrey 'prince of stinkers' Upjohn (Bertie's old headmaster) and Mrs Homer Cream, writer of crime fiction. Bertie's 'man' Jeeves is recalled from a holiday sampling the excellent shrimps at Herne Bay, to sort out the pickle that Bertie's meddling lands him in. Hence, for most of the novel Jeeves's presence and ultimate arrival is 'in the offing'.

Samuel de Champlain, the seventeenth-century navigator, cartographer and the 'Father of New France' (Canada) begins to give an idea of what 'the offing' actually is. In his eponymous *Voyages*, he described one location thus:

> *Rivierre Platte, coming from the mountains, only navigable for canoes. It is dry here at low tide a long distance out. Good anchorage in the offing.*

The 'offing' (sometimes 'offin') is a part of the sea, specifically the part that stretches from the coast to the horizon and can be seen from the shore. Therefore it has no fixed extent, but is dependent on location and circumstance. In modern terms we sometimes call it the littoral. Any ship in this area is said to be 'in the offing', i.e. might be about to make landfall or enter harbour, hence its arrival in such a place will happen in the near future. Ships that 'keep a good offing' keep well off the land while under sail to avoid navigational hazards that often lie close to shore.

The oggin

From 'offing' it's a very short voyage to 'the oggin', which is sailor slang for the sea. It could be derived from two possible sources. One theory is that the word 'ocean' was regularly mispronounced by sailors as 'oggin'. The second is that 'oggin' is a derived from 'hogwash' via 'og-wash'; hogwash being the rubbish swill fed to pigs which itself then became a slang term for nonsense. 'Oggin' is used most commonly afloat, particularly by the lower deck, and is rarely encountered these days by those unfamiliar with the sea or naval literature. To be '**floggin the oggin**' is to be at sea.

Which way the wind blows

You don't need a weather man
To know which way the wind blows
'Subterranean Homesick Blues' by Bob Dylan

Moving from water to air, there are several terms in use today relating to wind which have their origins in nautical slang. 'Taking the wind out of someone's sails' has previously been discussed, so let's see which way the wind is blowing with this particular subject.

It was imperative that sailors knew precisely from which direction and at what strength the wind was blowing. At times such knowledge simply allowed them to set the best sailing rig for the conditions and to plot a satisfactory course to the eventual destination. However, in times of peril, either in battle or in bad weather, the very lives of all on board ship could depend on precise calculations based on accurate reading of the wind.

In action having the wind in one's favour and being upwind of an enemy was called having the weather gauge. A fleet in such a position could attack or stand off a fleet downwind and hence could exert (in theory) more control over the outcome of the battle, for example the British Fleet under Admiral Lord Nelson had the weather gauge at the battle of Trafalgar allowing him to attack the combined Franco-Spanish fleet (even though the wind was quite light). In bad weather it was essential to know exactly where the wind was coming from; failure to react to changes in wind could damage a ship's masts and yards and even drive a ship onto the shore where she would be smashed to pieces.

Therefore to see 'which way the wind blows' is a phrase used when judging a situation to ascertain the course, the likely outcome and to use that information to make an informed decision.

Whistle up a/the wind

This phrase is used ashore to describe an activity that is not entirely likely to succeed, or for those entertaining false hopes. Sailors did not whistle on board ship, primarily because it could be confused with the boatswain's call. The boatswain was the officer in charge of the sails, spars, rigging, cables, etc., on board ship. He would use a specific whistle to pipe the hands to their stations according to the orders he received from a superior. Superfluous whistling could therefore cause confusion, a potentially dangerous situation on a ship where safety involved prompt and accurate interpretation of orders. According to naval lore, the only other members of a ship's crew who were allowed whistle were the cooks; whistling while preparing and cooking food was evidence that they were not sneakily helping themselves to the sailors' grub!

There was one particular exception to this rule. As we all know, sailing ships need wind to provide propulsion. Sailors were a very superstitious bunch; they believed that in a becalmed situation the only way to raise a wind was to whistle for it, specifically by whistling in the direction of the wind that was desired, giving rise to the phrase 'whistling up a/the wind'. This might, eventually, have the desired effect, especially as sailing ships tended to follow recognised and regular trade winds. On the other hand, perhaps the ineffectiveness of this action led to the phrase being turned on its head when used ashore to suggest that 'whistling' for something will produce absolutely nothing. In other words, when a person asks for something but another person won't give it to them, the reply could be '**you can whistle for it**!'

Break the ice

> *Vivian (Julia Roberts): 'You know, you could pay me now, and break the ice.'*
> Pretty Woman

When one is attending a civilised gathering, a garden party, cocktail reception or maybe a formal dinner, it can sometimes be tricky to start up conversation with other guests. We don't know who they are, we might have nothing in common with them, we might make a fool of ourselves with stilted and embarrassing conversation. In such social situations it is often a good idea to find a way to 'break the ice', i.e. to remove the frosty, formal nature of the event and replace it with a more congenial atmosphere.

The phrase comes from the **ice breaker**, which is a specially adapted or designed ship used to force through ice, thereby making the passage easier for other vessels. In the classic age of sail polar exploration was carried out by bomb vessels (ships that were designed to bombard positions ashore) specially converted to include reinforced bows to break through pack ice. HMS *Erebus* and *Terror* are two examples of converted bomb vessels, which went to the Arctic with the ill-fated expedition of Sir John Franklin in 1845. During the nineteenth and twentieth centuries specialist ice-breaking ships were developed, including the 'North Star', an 1868 wooden construction horse-drawn icebreaker used to force a passage through the canals of England's Midlands. It now lies derelict at the Black Country Living Museum. Nowadays, modern vessels fulfil a multitude of roles beyond simple icebreaking; for instance, the US Coastguard's *Healy* can break ice 4.5 feet thick at a speed of 3 knots and also houses 4,200 square feet of laboratory space which acts as a mobile research platform. *Healy* can also perform support tasks such as search-and-rescue, environmental monitoring and protection and the enforcement of maritime laws.

In deep water

When most landlubbers hear this phrase they will think of inexperienced swimmers who find themselves at the wrong end of the local municipal swimming pool, or perhaps those who have swum into the sea a little too far. In such a situation panic can set in and the individual can sometimes be seen floundering. They are in deep water and also 'out of their depth', i.e. in a position of discomfort and potential peril. Yet there is more to being 'in deep water' than just finding one's feet don't touch the bottom. Like many nautical phrases it is a favourite device of the media to describe someone or something in a tricky situation. In April 2006 the UK's *Telegraph* newspaper reported on a wave of motorists who, on blithely following their GPS systems, had ended up stranded in 4 feet of water in the River Avon at the Wiltshire village of Luckton with the headline, 'Sat-nav Drivers Land in Deep Water Again'.

Sailors identify two types of water: inshore, fairly shallow coastal water and the deep water of the world's oceans. In his *Sailor's Word Book* Smyth defines deep water very precisely as any water with a depth greater than 20 fathoms. The differences between a voyage in coastal waters and one across the ocean are quite marked. Apart from the absence of shelter and psychological comfort provided by land, the sailor can encounter dangerous oceanic weather and sea conditions when in deep water. Oceanic storms can throw up enormous waves and this, coupled with the swell of the sea can literally swamp ships and send them to the bottom; anyone who has seen the film *The Perfect Storm* will appreciate this phenomenon. Therefore, to be 'in deep water' can mean to be in water of greater depth than one's own height and hence in danger of drowning, or it can mean to be in a situation of potential danger where one needs plenty of skill, experience and concentration (and no doubt a bit of luck) to navigate a safe passage.

With all this in mind, it is evident why *Deep Water* was selected as the title for the 2005 film version of the controversial 1968–9 solo 'Golden Globe Race' during which British competitor Donald Crowhurst faked log entries and radio positions for his 40ft trimaran *Teignmouth Electron*. The whole sham placed Crowhurst under immense psychological pressure. The fake entries required complex celestial calculations and, when coupled with the random collections of poems and other writings found aboard his boat, which amounted to more than 25,000 words, all indicate a man on the verge of madness. With his last log entry of 29 June 1969, it is assumed that Crowhurst ended the charade and his life by jumping overboard sometime shortly after that date.

On the rocks

Not to be confused with a drink served on ice, to be 'on the rocks' is to be washed up and broke. The phrase is a firm favourite of tabloid hacks when speculating about celebrity marriages or relationships that are in danger of breaking up.

All sailors know that rocks, especially those that are partly or completely submerged by tides, are extremely hazardous geological features. The River Tyne's Black Middens at Tynemouth were notorious in the nineteenth century. In one storm during November 1864 they accounted for the loss of five ships in just three days. Even worse were the infamous Eddystone Rocks, 9 miles off the Cornish and Devon coastline and the Bell Rock, 11 miles off the Firth of Tay on the East Coast of Scotland. It is no surprise that these two nefarious reefs were the sites of remarkable feats of engineering to erect lighthouses to warn ships of the danger. If a ship were to be driven onto these dangerous features, she would literally be 'on the rocks' and would begin to break up unless quickly moved off.

Tide over

To 'tide something over' is a term often used to describe the process of coming up with a temporary solution to a wider problem or a difficult period of time. For example, in *Little Dorrit*, Charles Dickens has Mr Arthur Clenham attempting to free Amy Dorrit's father William from Marshalsea debtor's prison. He seeks help from Mr Pancks and, after Clenham outlines the dire situation of the Dorrit family finances, Pancks asks:

> '*Is it impossible, sir, to tide over for the present?*'
> '*Out of the question. Nothing can be tided over now.*'

The phrase quite often takes monetary form; for instance, an advance on one's monthly salary would 'tide one over' until payday. The reference to monetary needs is quite pertinent, for to have enough money to get by is often referred to as '**keeping afloat**'.

The nautical origin of this term comes from the word 'tide'. 'Tiding over' is a complex sailing technique used to make some forward movement into a strong headwind, i.e. a wind (often called a 'foul wind') that is blowing from the direction of intended sailing. As it is reliant on the tidal movement of the sea it is obviously relevant in tidal areas, such as harbours, rivers and channels. According to Smyth it is 'to work up or down a river or harbour, with a fair tide in a head wind or a calm; coming to anchor when the tide turns'. In layman's terms this is using the natural flow of a tide to carry a vessel in the desired direction, when the tide flows against the desired course, the vessel anchors, thereby maintaining its new position and awaits the next tide to make further progress.

Under the weather

This commonly used phrase describes a non-specific feeling of illness; from a simple sniffle to more serious ailments such as an alcohol-induced malaise, i.e. a hangover.

Of course like many phrases it has entered popular culture because of this wide application to almost any feeling of sickness, from personal illness to wider problems afflicting the world at large. On her first album, Scottish singer-songwriter KT Tunstall included a song simply called 'Under the Weather'. In this she raises the issues surrounding the acceptability of perceived 'outsiders' in a multicultural society:

> *Coz I'm under the weather*
> *Just like the world*
> *So sorry for being so bold*
> *When I turn out the light*
> *You're out of sight*
> *Although I know that I'm not alone*
> *Feels like home*

Yet the term has a distinct and more precise meaning when used by sailors. For a start it is often used when referring to *mal-de-mer*, also known as seasickness, especially when it is experienced by landlubbers. As seasickness usually occurs due to bad weather condition creating choppy seas, often with thick, dark clouds overhead, the sufferer is literally 'under the weather' when feeling sick. Moreover, when the wind is really blowing hard and smashing waves into the side of a ship, that side is said to be '**under the weather bow**'.

Even some of history's greatest sailors have suffered from *mal-de-mer* from time to time. Writing to his 'Dearest' Emma Hamilton from HMS *Medusa*, stationed in the Downs, on 31 August 1801, Admiral Lord Nelson complained of the seasickness that afflicted him throughout his glorious career:

> *The weather is very bad, and I am very sea-sick. I cannot answer your letter, probably; but I am writing a line, to get on shore, if possible: indeed, I hardly expect that your letter can get afloat ... Oh! how bad the weather is!*

In a postscript he despaired:

> *I am so dreadfully sea-sick, that I cannot hold up my head!*

An albatross around one's neck

The thought of any individual having to carry an albatross draped around their neck like a seabird scarf might seem a little bizarre. Ashore the term is used to describe an annoying burden that one must carry. It could be a business venture which loses more money than it makes. The example below, discussing a car-manufacturing firm, from an article in *The Times*, October 2006, illustrates the point:

> *Jaguar's in such a bad state it can't even sell itself. Over the past few weeks it has been portrayed as a multi-billion-dollar albatross around the neck of Ford.*

The 'albatross' does not have to be a physical thing either, past actions which come back to affect current matters can also be described as an albatross around one's neck.

The original nautical usage refers to a punishment, which is explained in more detail below. But first one myth needs to cleared up; although sailors regarded the albatross with some suspicion, even believing them to be the spirits of sailors lost at sea, it did not stop them killing and eating these large, heavy seabirds!

It all began with Samuel Taylor Coleridge's *The Rime of the Ancient Mariner*, first published in 1798. In the poem the Ancient Mariner details his epic tale to the narrator. When his ship is hit by a storm it is driven south towards the pole and while adrift amongst the ice an albatross appears as a saviour, bringing a change in fortune. The ice splits and the ship sails free with the albatross apparently keeping watch over the lives of the crew. Then:

> *God save thee, ancient Mariner!*
> *From the fiends, that plague thee thus! –*
> *Why look'st thou so? – With my cross-bow*
> *I shot the ALBATROSS.*

This act brings misfortune upon the ship as the wind drops and she drifts into the **doldrums** (see above). After more mishaps, the Ancient Mariner blames all the bad luck on his actions:

> *Ah! well a-day! what evil looks*
> *Had I from old and young!*
> *Instead of the cross, the Albatross*
> *About my neck was hung.*

Of course, the only people who would like to have an albatross around their neck on a regular basis are golfers; an albatross is any score three under par.

4

BIGWIGS AND MATELOTS

At sea the sailor lived a highly structured life. The ship's crew was divided up into specific groups depending on their roles. At a simple level, for the majority of ships that ran a two-watch system, most of the crew would be divided into starboard and larboard (or port) watches. This basic categorisation defined how the sailor would spend his day. Operating according to that basic division, men were classified as to where they worked. On a sailing warship the most highly skilled sailors would be the topmen; those who worked in the rigging and on the sails. This required a good deal of experience and knowledge. They were divided into those men who worked in the fore, main and mizzen tops. The rest did not tend to work aloft and were usually stationed in the forecastle or were the afterguard; the men who worked the poop and quarterdecks. So, for example, a man could be a fore topman in the starboard watch and he would have a similar person fulfilling this role in the larboard watch. The system ensured that there would always be enough men on duty to sail the ship at any one time. The remainder of the crew were classified as 'idlers', who men fulfilled a variety of duties. For instance the sailmaker, the armourer, the cooper and all their mates were all classified as 'idlers'. They did not keep the night watch, but could be called on at any time to work if the situation required them. When sail gave way to steam, a new classification system was implemented to include the new duties; for example the designation of 'stoker' for those men shovelling coal into the boilers.

Ranked above the men were petty officers, such as the master-at-arms or the boatswain's mates (perhaps the most feared men on board as they were responsible for 'encouraging' the hands). Each ship would also have a number of midshipmen. These were mostly young men beginning their careers at sea. If he passed the relevant exam, the young man could (it was not guaranteed as positions were for a specific ship) be promoted to lieutenant. He would now be a commissioned officer and might, if given the right circumstances, make it to captain. This was the hardest step in an officer's career. If he was lucky and made captain, promotion would come entirely by seniority, i.e. it would depend on the date he was posted to captain. A captain could be ranked as a commodore, a temporary position to allow a junior officer with promise to take control of a squadron. Moving upwards from this there was the rather complicated system of vice, rear and full admirals, the former two also being subdivided into red, white and blue categories.

With his position in the naval hierarchy defined, until 1805 the sailor's day ran from midday to midday, though nowadays it runs from midnight to midnight. The day was divided into a number of specific periods of time, also called watches. They regulated which part of a ship's crew were on duty at any time and, from the serving of food, to time set aside for rest and sleep, the entire naval day revolved around them. Each watch was of four hours' duration, apart from two shorter 'dog watches'. This made the amount of watches in each day seven; an uneven number which ensured that no-one had to keep to the same watch pattern. This not only shared the burden of the more unpopular watches in a fair manner, but also provided some variation in the daily experience of living and working aboard a man-of-war. In the Royal Navy the watches were organised as follows:

12:00 – 16:00   Afternoon Watch: At 12:00 the ship's position would be taken and recorded in the log book. The sailors would also receive their main meal of the day. The rest of the afternoon would be spent in maintenance if needed.

16:00 – 18:00   First Dog Watch: Supper would sometimes be served around 16:00, on some ships later at 19:00.

18:00 – 20:00   Last Dog Watch.

20:00 – 00:00   First Watch: Those not on watch would go to their hammocks. All lights would be extinguished during the hours of darkness.

00:00 – 04:00   Middle Watch: The most unpopular watch, also called the Graveyard Shift.

04:00 – 08:00   Morning Watch: On many ships the morning hours were spent cleaning and scrubbing decks. At 08:00 all hands would be piped to breakfast.

08:00 – 12:00   Forenoon Watch: Maintenance and exercise usually took place during these hours. Any punishments would be meted out around 11:00 after the crew were inspected.

The passage of time on board ship was marked by the striking of a bell every half hour. Therefore a strike of eight bells would signify the passage of four hours and signal the end of a watch. There would always be some of the crew on duty, lookouts, and a helmsman and so on. Yet, within this regimented day there would be time set aside for the men for exercise and education, with of course some time for leisure and relaxation.

Bigwig

When we think of a 'bigwig' we imagine a person in a position of responsibility – perhaps the managing director of a company, a VIP, or a member of what we call 'the establishment': Members of Parliament, Congressmen and Senators, Lords, Judges and so on. Wigs, nowadays, are the preserve of the British judiciary, ageing lotharios, and certain celebrities.

Three hundred years ago it was all very different; any person of note was expected to wear a wig as it was a sign of acceptability, respectability and of position in society. In nineteenth-century France the size of the wig was an important sign of power and prestige and as a consequence wigs became huge! As many countries followed the trends set by Parisian society, the practice became widespread amongst European nobility. Contemporary imagery would often caricature such people with underdeveloped craniums topped off with ridiculously oversized wigs. Dickens described the Bigwig family in *Nobody's Story* as 'composed of all the stateliest people thereabouts, and all the noisiest'. The attire of any sea officer of importance would not be complete without a wig of considerable size. Hence, among the lower-deck officers these 'important' officers would be known as 'bigwigs', a name that has stuck to this day for high-ranking persons.

Flimsy

The word 'flimsy' is used to describe anything that is thin, weak, without substance or not quite up to the task. A flimsy excuse is one that is likely to be seen through. Many news sources have used the word to describe the British Government's pre-war dossier on Iraq's weapons of mass destruction once it came to light that key sections were assembled by relatively junior staff. During the Hutton inquiry into the death of weapons expert Dr David Kelly, the UK's *Independent* newspaper stated:

> *Perhaps the most damning evidence to emerge from the Hutton inquiry is the fact that the Government knew exactly how flimsy its case was, but chose to keep its doubts to itself.*

The nautical connection to the word comes from the name given to the certificates of conduct that the commander of a ship would provide for any officer 'turning over', that is moving from one ship to another. These certificates would include details of the service dates of the officer, ranks attained and general comments from the commander as to the competence of the officer involved. In the nineteenth century the Royal Navy 'flimsy' also included details of height, hair and eye colour, complexion and distinguishing features, including tattoos. They also included a red triangle at the top right-hand corner which declared:

> *The corner of this Certificate is only to be cut off when the Character of the Man has been so bad as to make it desirable to prevent his re-entry into the Navy – any such case of a Continuous Service Man is to be specially reported.*

The paper used for these certificates was of a particularly thin nature – resembling thin film, the latter word being adapted into the term 'flimsy'. According to Covey Crump any officer appearing before a court martial could produce his flimsies to provide evidence of previous good character.

More recently the term 'flimsy' was used in the newspaper business, similarly to the naval origin of the word, it meant thin paper used by reporters to prepare their copy for eventual publication. The thin paper would allow carbon paper to be inserted between sheets and to produce multiple copies; the juxtaposition of 'flimsy' and the journalistic profession has not escaped the pen of many a wag.

Skipper

> *'By masts and keels! He takes me for the hunchbacked skipper of some coasting smack.'*
>
> Captain Ahab in *Moby Dick* by Herman Melville

Over a century-and-a-half after Melville wrote these words, the term skipper is still used to describe the captain of certain types of ship, in particular fishing boats and other privately owned or commercial craft. Therefore a skipper is the person in command of a ship, essentially an informal word for the captain. Admiral Smyth's definition that skipper is 'a man-of-war's man's constant appellation for his own captain' conveys the feeling of affection often underlying the relationship between a skipper and his crew.

These days the word 'skipper' is synonymous with the captain of a sports team, and the word is also repeatedly used when referring to the manager of a baseball team.

The very informality of the term has led to its widespread use among those of a non-naval or non-professional seafarer background who command such ships, whether they are commercial vessels or pleasure craft. The captain or skipper of a vessel has overall command and responsibility for everything that happens on board.

The word derives from the Dutch for ship, *schip*, hence *schipper* was used for those in command of a ship and became anglicised as skipper. The first sporting use of the word may have occurred in Scotland where it is still used for the captain of a curling team.

The rank of skipper entered the Royal Navy in 1911 with the Royal Naval Reserve (Trawler Section), created for mine-clearing duties. Perhaps the most famous skipper in the RNR was Thomas Crisp, VC. Crisp was awarded his posthumous VC for the defence of his command HM Armed Smack *Nelson* while under attack from the German U-boat *C-41*. The action, in all its gory detail, was reported in the *Supplement to the London Gazette*, 20 November 1918 (13695):

> *On the 15th August, 1917, the Smack 'Nelson' was engaged in fishing when she was attacked with gunfire from an enemy submarine. The gear was let go and the submarine's fire was returned. The submarine's fourth shot went through the port bow just below the water line and the seventh shell struck the skipper, partially disembowelling him, and passed through the deck and out through the side of the ship. In spite of the terrible nature of his wound Skipper Crisp retained consciousness, and his first thought was*

to send off a message that he was being attacked and giving his position. He continued to command his ship until the ammunition was almost exhausted and the smack was sinking. He refused to be moved into the small boat when the rest of the crew were obliged to abandon the vessel as she sank, his last request being that he might be thrown overboard.

In the mid-1980s the US navy named a short-range laser-guided missile 'Skipper' (AGM-123A *Skipper II*, based on the *Paveway II* Laser Guided Bomb), though the name was derived from the missile's flight path that often resembled a stone being 'skipped' across a pond. The missile was air-launched and designed for an anti-shipping role; it had a speed of 680mph and could deliver its 1000lb warhead at an effective range of 13.5 nautical miles. The 'Skipper II' (there was never a 'Skipper I') was phased out of service in the mid-1990s.

The word 'captain' itself is derived from the Italian *capitano*, which developed into *kapatan* or *kaptan* (over everything) and then became anglicised, perhaps through the French *capitaine* as captain. Note: although 'skipper' and 'captain' describe the same type of position, a skipper is not necessarily a captain, or vice versa, and using the words interchangeably can cause great offence amongst seafarers.

Blazer

Most people tend to have a love-hate relationship with the blazer jacket. For many it brings back memories of misspent youth; blazers were (and still are) a common uniform requirement for many schoolchildren. For others, the blazer can be an essential part of their wardrobe: ex-servicemen take pride in displaying their past career through the selection of an appropriate badge to display on their blazer. On the negative side it is the sign of a certain type of male, perhaps over fifty, who proudly takes up a minor position of power within their local community, and then, almost immediately, suffers from what one might call the 'Napoleon' or 'Little Hitler' syndrome, which is usually characterised by officious, patronising, pompous and misogynistic behaviour. The blazer is also much favoured by US television sports presenters.

The blazer has provided inspiration for two great British comic creations. Steve Coogan combined several of the above traits to produce a comedy giant, Alan Partridge, who in one TV episode tries to sell his very own sports tie and blazer badge sets. Perhaps even greater was *Fawlty Towers'* permanent resident and proud blazer wearer, Major Gowen, the dotty ex-soldier with a penchant for cricket, gin, colourful and racist language and losing his newspaper.

The blazer is a short double-breasted sports jacket, traditionally of navy blue, with green and a variety of striped colours also being popular, the latter especially amongst the sailing and boating community. But what is the source of the very strange name for this article of such sartorial mirth? Most sources point to a Captain J. W. Washington. In 1845, a few years before the naval uniform for ratings was brought in, Washington apparently decided that his boat crew should wear a rather fancy **rig**. This either consisted (the sources disagree on this point) of a snazzy blue or blue-and-white striped jacket (and one even mentions a blue-and-white striped pullover). As so often happens in the world of high fashion, the trend caught on. Washington's ship at the time was HMS *Blazer* – a wooden paddle sloop, built in 1834 and converted to a survey vessel in 1843 – thereby giving the world the blazer jacket. The current HMS *Blazer* is a 54-ton P2000 Class Patrol Vessel and is part of the University of Southampton's Royal Naval Unit.

Admiral

If a naval officer reaches the rank of admiral then he can certainly judge his career to be a success. It is the highest rank, though there are subdivisions within it. Famous Admirals include Horatio Nelson (RN), Chester Nimitz (USN) Tōgō Heihachirō (Japan) and Nikolai Kuznetsov (USSR). The most senior rank was Admiral of the Fleet, the naval equivalent of Field Marshal in the Army. The first admiral of the fleet in the Royal Navy was Edward Russell, the 1st Earl of Orford, appointed in 1690, but in 1996 the rank fell out of favour. In the United States Navy the term used is Fleet Admiral, a five-star rank, but it is only used in time of war.

Ashore, many companies, from a sportswear manufacturer to an insurer, have decided to use the word to convey an air of distinction and respectability. Then, of course, there is the frozen admiral's pie – a tasty concoction of Alaskan pollock and butter sauce topped off with mashed potato (in the true spirit of research the author consumed one during the writing of this book).

The word originated in the Near East, coming from the Arabic for Lord of the Seas, *Emir-el-Bahr*. Crusading Christian knights brought the term back with them, becoming *amiral* in French and *admiralis* in Latin with the first occurrence of the anglicised word 'admiral' dating from the late thirteenth century. The Admiralty building in Whitehall is still used by Government today, although the administration of the Royal Navy now falls under the remit of the Ministry of Defence.

The populous Red Admiral butterfly (*Vanessa atalanta*) is found throughout the world, from as far north as Canada, through Europe, Northern Africa to as far south as New Zealand and as far east as Iran. It has a distinctive red-orange band across the wing, which, as they are similar to the chevrons on a naval uniform, gives it its name.

Matelot

This strange word is an affectionate name for fellow sailors. It should not be confused with mate, which refers to an assistant, such as boatswain's mate or carpenter's mate. *Matelot* (pronounced mat-low) is the French word for sailor and is seemingly derived from *mattennoot*, the Middle Dutch for bed mate.

Flogging a dead horse

This familiar phrase has widespread use ashore. It is used in reference to a vain attempt to revive interest in something or to try something that has little chance of success. In the Coen brothers' 2004 remake of the classic 1955 Ealing Studio caper *The Ladykillers*, Professor G.H. Dorr expresses his growing frustration with his inept fellow crooks and attempts to explain a plan for stealing money:

> 'And what, to flog a horse that if not at this point dead is in mortal danger of expirin', does the dotted square represent?'

Obviously, flogging a dead horse in an attempt to make it work would be a completely fruitless exercise. The phrase originates from the custom of paying in advance for work. This most often occurred at sea when a sailor signed onto a new ship. He would be paid in advance a month or two worth of wages, which tended to be quickly and easily spent on booze, gambling and women while the ship prepared to sail. This would lead to a period of time at sea which the sailors would consider as working for nothing. Moreover, the captain and officers would find any attempt to cajole the men to enter enthusiastically into laborious activity during this period a rather hopeless exercise; this led to the modern-day use of the term for a futile undertaking.

But where does the horse reference come from? There is an old seafaring custom whereby when the period without pay was over, i.e. the men were earning money again, they would celebrate by dragging a canvas horse effigy, stuffed with straw, round the decks and running it up the yard arm. The horse symbolised the sailor's 'fruitless labour' during what they called the 'horse period'. It was then destroyed in symbolic fashion by cutting the cable and letting it fall into the sea – all accompanied by much hilarity and chanting. The horse effigy itself appears to have originated with the Spaniards. For ships heading to the Americas or to the Indies, the horse period often seems to have ended in an area of calm around 30°–35° north of the equator. This was a well-known phenomenon and ships becalmed in this hot, muggy belt might throw overboard excess animals, such as horses, to conserve water and lighten the load. This area was known to Spanish crews as the 'Gulf of the Mares' and then by English speakers as the 'horse latitudes'. Reaching these latitudes coincided with the end of the period of time during which the captain would be 'flogging a dead horse' if he tried to get his men to work harder.

Rig

A sailors 'rig' is his dress, his various outfits. For instance, the Royal Navy currently has blue and white uniforms, each subdivided into different rigs: Formal Dress/Undress (No. 1 Dress), Formal Evening Dress/Undress (No. 2 Dress), General Duty Rig (No. 3 Dress) and the Blue Uniform and Improved Action Working Dress (IAWD No. 4 and No. 5). In 1955 when Covey Crump published his work on naval slang he remarked that the 'Rig of the Day' was the, 'naval name for the type of uniform directed to be worn each day; it is piped at breakfast time in each ship daily'. Nowadays the default dress for the Royal Navy is No. 3 (General Duty) unless otherwise specified.

In the days of sail a sailor would have to pay for his clothes, as before 1857 there were no standard uniforms for the men. If he had been **press-ganged** (see Chapter 5), the sailor might only have the clothes he was wearing when seized. Despite the lack of uniforms, sailors tended to favour certain styling to their clothes. While long coats, breeches and stockings might have been suitable for those ashore, on board ship they would have been completely impractical. So the sailor favoured a short jacket, checked shirts and loose-fitting trousers that could be rolled up, thereby giving him a distinctive look. His clothing would usually consist of his everyday working rig plus, if at all possible, a smart, best outfit for a run ashore, known as his shore rig. Some officers tried to achieve some consistency by limiting the men to certain choices; blue jackets, white trousers, and so on. The round narrow-brimmed hat was common, which in some cases carried the ship's name in capital lettering across the front. The sailor was also attracted to colourful and garish ornamentation, silver watches and silver buckles for shoes being a common extravagance. Therefore to be **'rigged out'** in your finest is to be dressed up in your best clothes.

'Rigging' has also been used to describe the fitting or fixing up of something. On board ship the rigging is the cordage, masts, spars and sails, which all provide forward propulsion to the ship. The actual arrangement of the rig would differ between ships, for instance a square-rigged ship would have a completely different set-up from a ship rigged fore and aft.

The word 'rig' could derive from any number of sources: the old Anglo-Saxon *wrigan* – to clothe; the Scandinavian *rigga/rigge* – to set up the rigging on board ship; the Middle English *rig* – to bind/wrap.

Whatever the origin, the definition that is most common ashore relates to clothing. In *Anne of Green Gables*, Marilla Cuthbert pokes fun at the title character, the 11-year-old Anne Shirley:

'Anne, Mrs Rachel says you went to church last Sunday with your hat rigged
out ridiculous with roses and buttercups. What on earth put you up to such
a caper?'

In the mid-nineteenth century a former inmate of Dartmoor prison
reminisced about the state of dress during his incarceration. The uniform
consisted of woollen jacket and pantaloons, dyed bright yellow and marked
with upright arrows:

> *… nothing could exceed the grotesqueness of appearance of an individual
> rigged out in this garb of captivity.*
>
> The United States Magazine and Democratic Review, 1846

Cut of his jib

While on the subject of appearances, this famous saying is widely used
ashore to describe the way someone looks. As John Russell Bartlett stated in
his 1848 book *Dictionary of Americanisms: A glossary of Words and Phrases
Usually Regarded as Peculiar to the United States*:

> *The form of his profile, the cast of his countenance; as, 'I knew him by the
> cut of his jib.' A nautical vulgarism.*

The jaunty yet familiar nature of the phrase makes it a favourite of comedy
writers, for instance Cliff Clavin's use of the term in a 1982 episode of the
sit-com *Cheers*:

> *'Yeah, I know who this is. It's a tootsie on my route who's been eyeing the cut
> of my jib through her Levelors. Yeah, old man's probably out of town, she's
> looking for a little C.O.D.: Cliffy On Demand.'*

Or *The Simpsons'* Mr Burns, who used it in two episodes from 1989:

> *'Hmm … who's that goat-legged fellow? I like the cut of his jib.'*

And…

> *'Hold the phone, Smithers. I like the cut of your jib.'*

Originally, the term related to a precise feature on a person: their nose. This was because when, viewed in profile, the human nose vaguely resembles the outline of the large, triangular foremost sail on a sailing ship – the jib sail. Sailors could identify the nationality of a ship from quite a distance based on the different types of rig and the different sizes of the jib sail and decide whether they were friend or foe. For instance, French ships would often have their jib cut more acutely, making them instantly recognisable. So, sailors would use the phrase specifically to describe the expression on a person's face – whether they liked or disliked the 'cut of his jib'.

Slops/sloppy

Continuing the clothing theme, 'slops' were the various forms of ready-made clothing, hats, shoes, breeches, stockings etc., sold to sailors from the slop room on board ship.

The Royal Navy did not institute a formal uniform until 1857 and so prior to that a sailor just embarking on a career at sea would not have had clothing suited to the rigours of life at sea. When slops were introduced in 1623, the cheap, one-size-fits-all approach to manufacturing made things easy for naval suppliers and pursers. As civilian clothes wore out and were replaced with 'slops' it inevitably led to many sailors getting '**rigged out**' (see above) in ill-fitting, baggy garments; this was the genesis of the unofficial naval uniform that set sailors apart from shore-based society and would be formalised in 1857.

The word 'slop' derives from a specific piece of clothing, the old English *sloppe*, which were loose breeches. John Ogilvie's *A Supplement to the Imperial Dictionary* of 1855 defines slops as 'Wide Dutch breeches, introduced into England during the reign of Elizabeth'. And over 300 years before Ogilvie, John Palsgrave in his 1530 *L'esclaircissement de la langue Francoyse* translated 'sloppes, hosyn' as '*brayes à marinier*'. Due to the nature of slops the words 'slops' and 'sloppy' have acquired a derogative meaning, often used to describe rubbish or a careless, untidy approach to work. Shakespeare's Don Pedro in *Much Ado About Nothing* alludes to the questionable fashion sense of Germans:

> *There is no appearance of fancy in him, unless it be a fancy that he hath to strange disguises; as, to be a Dutchman today, a Frenchman to-morrow, or in the shape of two countries at once, as, a German from the waist downward, all slops, and a Spaniard from the hip upward, no doublet.*

Hand

A sailor, quite naturally, uses his hands an awful lot in his everyday work, hauling on ropes, climbing the rigging and so on, hence members of a ship's crew became known as 'hands'. Today we have many phrases which contain this word and are used with a nod to their original nautical origins, so it would be appropriate to consider some of them here:

'A dab hand': These days someone who is a dab hand at something is considered an expert in a particular field. For instance a chef might be considered a dab hand with a pan, or a painter a dab hand with a brush. In fact, this latter example is extremely pertinent.

On board a sailing ship there was an awful lot of painting to do. Before the Battle of Trafalgar many of the British ships were repainted with the famous 'Nelson chequer', two or three broad bands of yellow paint around the hull

with the lids of the gun ports painted black to create the chequerboard pattern. On 10 October 1805 Captain Duff of the 74-gun HMS *Mars* wrote to his wife:

> *I am sorry the rain has begun tonight, as it will spoil my fine work, having been employed for this week past to paint the ship à la Nelson, which most of the Fleet are doing.*

The sailors who would undertake painting duties as part of their workload would become rather good at painting and were known as '**dab-hands**'. In *Ship to Shore* Peter Jeans surmises this could come from the Latin for skilled – *adeptus*, and the practice of *daubing* houses with mud or clay on top of a wattle framework.

In the years before the Second World War the Royal Navy implemented a radical colour scheme, which varied the shade of grey according to where they were stationed:

East Indies – White
Mediterranean – Light Grey
China Station – Light Grey
Home Fleet – Dark Grey
Reserve Fleet – Very dark grey

Admiralty-issue grey paint was called 'Pusser's Crabfat' by the men, and while painting an entire ship in a drab grey sounds rather boring, there was one set of painters who had a more interesting task. These dab hands were the men who painted the 'Razzle Dazzle' camouflage schemes on ships during both World Wars. The striking colour schemes, the brainchild of artist Norman Wilkinson, consisted of a bizarre looking array of coloured (usually black, white, blue and green) geometric patterns (usually curved or striped) block painted onto the sides of a ship. Despite seemingly drawing attention to the ship, the patterns were designed to confuse enemy rangefinders thereby making it difficult to judge the ship's speed and range. (Such calculations were necessary in any gunnery or torpedo attack.) As Wilkinson himself admitted, it was designed to mislead the enemy rather than hide the ship. He explained the thinking behind the concept:

> *… to produce an effect by paint in such a way that all accepted forms of a ship are broken up by masses of strongly contrasted colour, consequently*

making it a matter of difficulty for a submarine to decide on the exact
course of the vessel to be attacked.

A striking example of adopting a colour scheme suitable for the prevalent
conditions comes from the ships of the Royal Navy's 3rd Escort Group
operating out of Iceland during the Second World War. Their biggest threat
was from enemy submarines, which usually operated at dawn or twilight,
and so the RN ships were painted pink to blend in with the colours of the
sky at these times of day. Nowadays the ships of most navies are painted a
uniform light grey – which makes for very dull viewing.

Hand over hand/fist: Two slightly different phrases with the same meaning:
to do something rapidly and continuously. They derive from the actions of
hauling on ropes or climbing up or down rigging. The very action of
hauling involved the movement of one free hand over the other hand while
that hand gripped the rope to maintain a continuous pulling action on the
rope or a continuous upward movement. Regarding the climbing of
rigging, an experienced sailor could climb, spider-like, up the complex
arrangement of rigging with immense speed, a process requiring a high
level of skill and accuracy. The term was then applied to any rapid progress,
for instance making money 'hand over fist'.

An old hand: An 'old hand' is literally a sailor with more experience than
younger 'green' sailors. His very age and knowledge mark him out and he is,
according to Smyth, 'A knowing and expert person'.

All hands to the pumps: During sailing, part of a ship is always beneath the
waves. In the age of sail most ships accumulated what is termed **bilge water**
(see Chapter 9), water ingress which, due to gravity, collected in the hold. If
not checked, this extra water could have a detrimental effect upon the
sailing properties of a ship. In stormy weather the inflowing water could
reach alarming proportions. If an excess of water entered below the
waterline, perhaps from grounding, enemy action or, in wooden ships, leaky
seams, the ship might capsize and sink.

Some ships were notoriously leaky; for instance the six ships of the Royal
Navy's *Endymion* class frigates built of fir, rather than traditional oak, in
1812–14. In *The Ionian Mission* Patrick O'Brian has Jack Aubrey posted to
the 74-gun HMS *Worcester*. The nature of this ship is detailed by her First
Lieutenant Thomas Pullings:

'*... she is more what we call a floating coffin than a ship. And as for the damp, what do you expect? She was built in Sankey's yard, one of the Forty Thieves: twenty-year-old wood and green stuff with the sap in it.*'

All ships had (and still do have) a series of pumps installed to pump out bilge water. A visitor can still see HMS *Victory*'s four chain pumps that operated from the lower gun deck and could remove 120 tons of water per hour. Chain pumps consisted of a series of small leather buckets attached to a long chain and contained within a copper or wooden tube. The contraption was operated by a winch handle which would turn the chain, thereby continuously filling the buckets and bringing them to a point where they emptied and sent the water over the side.

Obviously, operating these pumps was a strenuous activity and men tended to work in shifts if there was a lot of pumping to do; for instance if the hull had been holed. In a really dire situation, where a ship was in real danger of sinking, **all hands** could be called to **man the pumps** to eject water from the ship. And all hands meant everyone, even those usually excused from laborious duties such as the cook. Captain James Cook's *Endeavour* ran aground on coral reefs on Tuesday, 12 June 1770, and began to take in water. While trying to float the ship off the reef Cook noticed that the water ingress was becoming critical: 'This was an alarming and I may say terrible Circumstance'. With one of the ship's pumps not working the ship heaved off but with '3 feet 9 inches [of] water in the hold ... turn'd all hands to the Pumps the leak increasing upon us.' Eventually the leak was brought under control and the ship saved.

So in order to have all hands called to the pumps a ship must been in a very precarious state; that is how we use the phrase today, everyone must help out in a tricky situation.

Scuttle

This is a familiar term to all those with nautical yearnings. A scuttle is a small hole cut into either the deck (i.e. hatchways) or the sides of a ship. In fact the word 'scuttle' itself comes from the Spanish word for hatchway: *escotilla*. When such a hole is intentionally cut or bored into the sides below the waterline it can cause the ship to sink, hence the term for this process is '**scuttling**'. Perhaps the most famous example of scuttling is the intentional destruction of the German High Seas Fleet after the First World War: ten battleships, five battlecruisers, five cruisers and 32 smaller craft were sunk to prevent them being handed over to the British. So to scuttle something is to undermine, prevent or even sabotage an undertaking. On 11 April 2008 when the takeover of MacDonald Dettwiler & Associates by Alliant Techsystems was prohibited by the Canadian Government *The New York Times* covered the story with the headline, 'Two Issues Combine to Scuttle an Aerospace Takeover'.

Scuttlebutt

While on the topic of scuttling, the cask or butt holding fresh drinking water on the deck had a hole cut into the side of it to allow sailors access to water. This became known as 'the scuttlebutt'. The hole would be cut half way up the cask, ensuring that it would always be half full. As sailors would often congregate and linger around the cask, it was the place where gossip and rumour were exchanged and so the word 'scuttlebutt' entered the sailor's vocabulary. Unsurprisingly, 'The Scuttlebutt' is a title favoured by many yachting and sailing clubs and by the purveyors of damn fine, strong, navy-issue rum for their various newsletters.

One of the events often witnessed at Sea Scout regattas in the United States is the 'raising of the scuttlebutt', a competition in which teams construct a block and tackle tripod, hoist a 50-gallon cask of water to a height of three feet, lower it, break down the tripod and return to their starting positions. This process is completed three times and the team with the quickest time (under a minute is a good time) wins.

5

THE CAT

Warships need discipline to be effective instruments of war. But let's not get confused between discipline, which in naval terms was a code of conduct for the efficient running of a ship, and punishment, which is the actual term for that which is meted out to miscreants who have broken the rules. It is no surprise that a number of slang terms used ashore relate to punishments common in the age of sail. In time of war with large numbers of men mobilised and taken into the navy, maintaining discipline was absolutely vital. Yet, it must be seen in context. Society ashore could be quite a violent place, drunkenness, boisterous behaviour and fighting were commonplace and punishment ashore was usually harsher than that afloat.

In the Royal Navy the way a captain could run his ship was outlined in the Articles of War. These were a polyglot of rules and regulations dating back to the time of the Commonwealth in the 1650s and which acted as the basis for naval discipline. Amendments to the Articles were made in the eighteenth century, leaving the navy of Nelson's time with a core of 36 Articles. In the United States the military code dates to 1775 but was revised into the 1806 Articles of War which governed both the Navy and the Army.

In the Royal Navy's Articles of War offences were loosely divided into four categories: various forms of cowardice in the face of the enemy, for which the punishment was death; those dealing with offences against other persons, such as assault, murder and theft – the death penalty applied for some offences; offences against the King and his Government, espionage, working with the enemy, neglect of duty – in these cases punishment was again severe and the death penalty was often an option; a final group consisted of minor crimes against God or religion such as swearing – punishment was mild and ill-defined.

In every other case, it was up to the captain of a ship to decide how to punish breaches in discipline 'according to the laws and customs in such cases used at sea'. This was quite an open-ended statement, and could, on occasion, be open to abuse. It also left the captain in a difficult position. Every sailor on board a ship had a role to play and hence was a valuable resource, plus there were few arrangements for keeping men locked up. Courts martial could be convened but they required the presence of at least five captains; for ships operating alone or on long voyages this was hardly a viable option for all but the most serious crimes such as mutiny. Seamen had very few privileges that could be removed (perhaps the only real one was the grog ration) and all duties, even unpleasant ones, onboard a ship needed doing anyway.

In reality the only option open to captains was corporal punishment. This usually took one of two forms. The first was the informal and widespread punishment often called 'starting' whereby one of the petty officers would give a misbehaving or slovenly sailor a whack with a piece of rope. This was for minor offences and was open to serious misuse by vicious and vindictive officers.

Formal punishment came in the form of flogging, where the ship's company would be assembled on deck to watch miscreants have their backs cut open with the cat-o'-nine-tails. Offenders had usually committed some kind of offence that endangered themselves, the crew, the safety of the ship or fell into what we would now call 'anti-social behaviour'. Some offences, taken from the Black List (see page 72) of HMS *Blake* included:

Drunkenness (by far the most common offence) – punishment ranged from 'forgiven', presumably for first offences up to 12 lashes, then 24 for 'Repeated drunkenness'.
Stealing – various punishments to fit the crime, including stealing trousers 24 lashes, stealing trousers and money 36 lashes.
Filthiness, pissing out of the top – 12 lashes.
Neglect of duty – 12 lashes.
Striking the ropemaker – 6 lashes.
Quarrelling – 4 lashes.
Mutinous expressions – 24 lashes.

In addition, on the *Blake*'s Black List there was one instance of 'Attempting to violate a child, 7 years old' by Joseph Gregory, who received 24 lashes. The highest number of lashes recorded on the List was given to one James Mills who received three months confinement then 48 lashes for 'Attempting an unnatural crime with a boy'.

Under the Admiralty Regulations captains were only supposed to give out a maximum of 12 lashes. As it was hardly worth interrupting the workings of a ship to assemble the crew for anything less than that, they often exceeded the number – as evidenced by the *Blake*'s Black List. In Nelson's time most people agreed that it would have been impossible to abolish flogging, but many officers did actively try to limit its use. On board ship thieves were particularly harshly treated as theft had a hugely negative impact upon the morale of the crew. Thieves regularly received sentences of 200–500 lashes, although the full number were not necessarily carried out. Another offence that attracted severe punishment was sodomy, a death sentence could be handed out or at the least several hundred lashes. All contemporary opinion during the age of sail considered it the worst type of crime: one against God and nature.

Some captains took discipline to the extreme. Captain Hugh Pigot of the 32-gun frigate HMS *Hermione* certainly did. Pigot acquired a reputation as a brutal and violent officer: Dudley Pope called him 'possibly the cruellest Captain in the history of the service'. While patrolling in the West Indies in 1797 *Hermione* was hit by a squall on 20 September. Pigot ordered the topsails to be reefed with the caveat that the last man down would be flogged. With the men desperate to avoid punishment, three young sailors plummeted to their deaths on the decks below. Pigot ordered their bodies thrown overboard and had several dissenters beaten. With these acts Pigot had gone too far; the next day the men mutinied and hacked him to bits, casting his body parts into the sea.

Sailors could, and often did, have grounds to appeal, but in the main tended to be quite stoical about accepting punishment when they had committed an offence. James Cox, in HMS *Warspite* during the First World War, summed it up:

> *There's a lot to be said for discipline, because a well disciplined ship is usually a happy ship, because everybody knows they've got a job to do. In a badly disciplined ship, everybody pleases themselves.*

In the black books

In 1154 Henry of Anjou ascended to the throne of England bringing his wife, Eleanor of Aquitaine, with him. She, in turn, brought something with her: laws of the province of Aquitaine. These included those relating to the governance of the seafarers of the Island of Oleron situated in the Bay of Biscay, around 3km west of Rochefort. The Laws of Oleron were the first formal maritime laws in north-west Europe and were based upon existing maritime laws prevalent in the Mediterranean. The punishment of miscreants in the Laws of Oleron was pretty stern stuff by modern-day standards:

> *Whosoever shall commit murder aboard ship shall be tied to the corpse and thrown in to the sea. If a murder be committed on land, the murderer shall be tied to the corpse and buried alive.*

Anyone convicted of stabbing another person or of just drawing a knife 'shall loose [sic] a hand'.

Following Eleanor's arrival in England these maritime laws were gradually adopted, until in the mid-fourteenth century they began to be codified into a book called *Rules for the Office of Lord High Admiral; Ordinances for the Admiralty in Time of War; the Laws of Oleron for the Office of Constable and Marshall; and other Rules and Precedents.* As this book was bound with black or dark leather it became widely known as *The Black Book of the Admiralty*, a more catchy title. Apart from containing details of the appointments and conduct of cases at the High Court of Admiralty it also included a section on the punishment of offenders.

Once ashore the term '**black book**' spread to many other forms of law and from there to wider usage leading to the common meaning we have today; being 'in the black books' means to be in trouble, to have committed or given offence or to be in disgrace with another person because of one's actions or words.

Black list

The Black Book of the Admiralty is probably the source for another phrase we use ashore: 'black list'. Ashore a black list can be a list of names of people who are to be denied something, for example employment, privileges or access, either because of a transgression or because of their beliefs. Perhaps one of the most famous instances of **blacklisting** came in post-war America where the US Government set up the 'Un-American Activities Committee' and blacklisted several notable Hollywood personalities with perceived communist sympathies during the height of McCarthyism. It can also be applied to a black list of banned material, books for instance.

At sea the black list was the list of seamen who were due punishment – usually flogging. The Black List for HMS *Blake*, under the command of Captain Edward Codrington, shows 144 men flogged in fourteen months between 1811 and 1813, the vast majority for drink-related offences. By the First World War, with the age of flogging officially over, one of the typical punishments for those on the black list was scrubbing the decks or being assigned to other unpopular duties.

Press-ganged

This phrase has nothing to do with the early 1990s British children's TV series about a paper run by budding journalists. In fact it has nothing at all to do with the press or the journalistic profession.

To be press-ganged is to be coerced into doing some type of activity. Take this use of the term from Formula 1 Motor Racing boss Max Moseley when reminiscing about his student days at Oxford:

> *At Oxford … one was press-ganged into politics; people attack my father, so one had to defend him. But I can't pretend I didn't enjoy it.*

Of course one can't argue with the sentiment, but young Max's father was also the father of British Fascism, Oswald Moseley.

In times of war there were never enough experienced men to crew all the ships of the Royal Navy. In 1799 the navy needed a total of 120,000 men to provide crews for all its ships. To make up the shortfall the Admiralty ran the Impress Service. This consisted of organised groups of sailors under the leadership of an officer who would board other ships or go ashore in port towns to 'procure' experienced seamen of just about any nationality. A favoured trick of the Royal Navy was to board merchant ships which had just returned from overseas voyages because the men on board had nowhere to run. Such actions were usually carried out by individual gangs, rather than the Admiralty-authorised Impress Service. To avoid this form of impressment it soon became common practice for the crew of a returning vessel to go overboard into the ship's boats and row ashore, leaving the captain and officers to berth the ship. This could be done with the captain's consent.

Ashore, some men participated in the process by tempting sailors with booze, and getting them to sign up for service when under the influence. It was also common for the signatures to be forged, and the press-ganged man to wake up with a thick head on board ship! These men, who were paid money for each man they supplied, were known as 'crimps' and the money they received was referred to as 'blood money'. See also **Shanghai** later in this chapter.

Contrary to modern (and quite a bit of contemporary) popular belief, the press gangs did not set out to seize anyone they came across. What they were looking for were men of 'seafaring habits' between 18 and about 55. Men with little seafaring experience were of limited use onboard ship, what they were after were skilled mariners. Men taken into the service in this way were called 'pressed men' and were paid at a lower rate than those who had volunteered. The press-ganged men received a shilling upon their enrolment and it is from this act that the word *prest* derived, from the latin *praestare*, to warrant. The word became a bit jumbled up with *empresser*, to arrest, during the Middle Ages leaving us with 'pressed' describing the financial transaction rather than the act of coercion.

The Impress Service was hated by just about everyone, including some of those whose duties it was to impress men. Most commentators and artists show the service carrying out brutal acts to get the men necessary to ensure a full complement for their respective ships. Friction between the United States and Britain over the impressment of American nationals was one of the causes of the War of 1812. It certainly could be a risky job for all involved: on occasion press gangs would find themselves in street fights with locals. 'The Battle of Ballacraine' took place in the hotel of that name on the Isle of Man (a much favoured venue for the Impress Service due to the skilled sailors of the local herring fisheries). Ten Manx islanders fought off a dozen press-gang members, with one of the latter dying from his injuries.

The pressed man was contracted until the ship was paid off or the war ended, with the threat of the death penalty if they deserted. However, he had the right to appeal, and on more than one occasion the Admiralty overturned the decision to impress an individual. The one time that the rules on who could be taken were relaxed with official sanction was during a 'hot-press'. This was only implemented in times of real emergency, such as at the start of a war. During a hot-press anyone could find themselves in the hands of 'the

press', though the main targets were still experienced seamen. The deeply unpopular press was never used in Britain after the defeat of Napoleon.

Bootleg

Today we understand the word 'bootleg' to be something that is illegal: counterfeit cigarettes and clothing, fake DVDs, CDs, downloads of copyrighted music and video material and so on. Such goods are sold on the black market at a fraction of the price of the originals. The term came to international prominence during the era of Prohibition in the United States 1919–33. With alcohol outlawed, the black market for smuggled and illegally brewed booze fell under the control of the major crime syndicates. One popular way around both of these problems was implemented by American sailors, themselves often rather partial to the odd tipple: smuggling booze into the country by the beautifully simple measure of concealing it in the top of their heavy leather sea boots. Any sailor indulging in this practice was therefore a '**bootlegger**'.

Perhaps one of the most famous bootleggers was Florida-based Captain William S. McCoy. Instead of hiding his illegal booze, in this instance rum, in his boots, he hid it in his boat, the *Tomika*, specially adapted to conceal as much liquor as possible and armed with a machine gun to ward off any interfering US Coast Guards. Many rum-runners allegedly watered down their bootleg goods to maximise profits but, according to popular rumour, William McCoy never did. His stuff was the genuine article, one possible origin of the term '**the real McCoy**'.

Run the gauntlet

In October 2007, the UK's *The Times* ran an article describing how American treasure hunters had almost clashed with a Spanish warship off the coast of Gibraltar with the headline: 'Treasure seekers Run the Gauntlet over World's Biggest Haul of Gold'. In modern-day usage to 'run the gauntlet' is to be attacked or threatened with attack – physically or metaphorically – simultaneously from all sides.

This does bear some relation to the origins of the term; for in the past if you were 'running the gauntlet' you would find it a very painful process. It was a punishment originating in Sweden, but is perhaps most famously used in the Royal Navy. It was particularly favoured by ships' captains when faced with a case of robbery. Stealing from ship mates was a serious offence; it impacted upon the morale of the crew as sailors suspected one another of the crime. Hence, when the thief was eventually caught, retribution involved the whole of the ship's crew. The **hands** were assembled into parallel lines through which the offender would be walked by two officers, one in front walking backwards with a drawn cutlass to prevent the miscreant from passing through too fast, and one behind to ensure there was no slowing down. As the thief passed each man he was beaten with a plaited rope yarn.

The word 'gauntlet' in this case has nothing to do with the form of armoured glove used in the Middle Ages, and from where we have the phrase 'throwing down the gauntlet'. Instead in this case 'gauntlet' has a Swedish origin, from the word for 'street run', '*gatlopp*'. This was a form of military and civilian punishment similar to the Royal Navy's version. The term and practice seem to have spread to the British Isles through British mercenaries serving with Swedish troops in the Thirty Years War (1618–48). The original word *gatlopp* became anglicised with many variations including gantlet, gantelope as well as gauntlet.

Over a barrel

To be 'over a barrel' is, like many of the phrases in this chapter, to be in a rather tricky situation. The person over the barrel is at a disadvantage compared with the person who has placed them in that position. In extreme circumstances the person over the barrel can be entirely at the mercy of another. It is a favourite phrase of commentators discussing any increases in the cost of oil or of authors writing more extended pieces about the various problems facing the world's oil markets. For instance in *The Economist* on 8 November 2007: 'Over a Barrel: Rising Oil Price Equals Rising Profits, Right? Wrong' or this from the *Washington Post* in October 2006: 'Africa over a Barrel'. Tom Mast and Raymond J. Learsay both used the phrase for books about oil published in 2005.

There are two possibilities for the origin of the term: that a barrel was used in life-saving or a barrel was used in punishment. In the former case many laymen believed that a barrel could be used as a primitive resuscitation device for those pulled lifeless from water. With the victim suitably placed over the barrel they would then be repeatedly rolled backwards and then forwards in the hope that the motion would eject water from the unfortunate's stomach. However, *The Angler's Guide* of 1815, which included a handy section on life-preserving techniques for those anglers who found a colleague in the water, suggested otherwise:

In removing the body to a convenient place, care must be taken that it be not bruised, nor shaken violently, nor roughly handled, nor carried over any man's shoulders with the head hanging downward, nor rolled upon the ground, nor over a barrel, nor lifted up by the heels; for experience proves, that all these methods may be injurious, and destroy the small remains of life.

This belief was backed up by some rather bizarre empirical medical evidence. In 1775 a Dutch surgeon, P. Beije, stopped bystanders rolling a boy called Cornelis Bijl over a barrel after retrieving him from the water in the town of Zierikzee. Instead Beije took the extraordinary measure of blowing smoke up the boy's backside while rubbing his stomach in an attempt to stimulate his lungs. Miraculously the boy coughed up the water and eventually made a full recovery and Beije was awarded a silver medal from the Society for Rescuing the Drowned in Amsterdam.

Ashore the use of a barrel in punishment seems quite widespread. In the American South, during the days of slavery, the use of a wooden barrel in administering punishment was commonplace as recalled by one ex-slave Hagar: 'Don't done you task, driver wave that whip, put you over the barrel, beat you so blood run down'. Or take the court case (from 1827) of the commander of an English merchant ship that had put into the Russian port of Odessa. One of the Seamen had committed an act of mutiny on board the

ship, and the commander had sent him ashore under the guard of Russian soldiers to be incarcerated. He was then 'taken out of prison by the Russian officers and soldiers, thrown over a barrel and flogged'.

The naval usage of the phrase has a slightly different slant with regard to punishment. For certain offences the miscreant would be draped over a cannon barrel, ready to receive a number of lashes. So in this instance it is a gun barrel, and not a wooden cask barrel, that is at the nub of the issue. This method of punishment was also known as 'kissing' or 'marrying the gunner's daughter'; a gunner's daughter being the actual cannon barrel. This form of punishment was not very common and more usually reserved for misbehaving midshipmen and the device used across their backsides would be a cane, not **the cat** (see later). The regular sailor would receive his lashes across his back from the infamous cat-o'-nine-tails tied to a grating on deck where everyone could see and though, not technically 'over a barrel', he would be in a grim situation.

Hijack

To be hijacked is to have someone else take control by the use or threatened use of force; it is usually associated with major news stories, in particular the hijacking of airliners by terrorists. Although the first recorded aircraft hijacking occurred in 1960, it was the 1976 hijacking of an Air France flight and the subsequent anti-terrorist operation at Entebbe airport in Uganda that set the tone for over two decades of politically motivated hijackings. The hijacking of aircraft entered a new and deadly phase with the terrorist attacks of 9/11. Hijacking is also used in the world of computing, describing when malicious individuals use spyware and virus software to effectively gain control of another person's or organisation's computing equipment.

For the naval connection this old salty story possibly gives the answer. Sailors on shore leave would often be looking for some form of 'entertainment'. In ports frequented by American sailors, ladies of the night would hail their potential clients with the alluring call 'Hi Jack'. With the gleeful sailor ready to fulfil his part of the deal a third party would clock him over the head and either rob him of his money or sell him onto a ship in need of extra hands. The use of subterfuge and violence following the initial 'Hi Jack' has therefore passed into general usage.

Keelhauled

This is one of those phrases that is often used ashore without much thought as to the barbarism of the original act. When people use the phrase today they are usually referring to some form of verbal reprimand, such as being told off by one's boss and is such cases they often drop the 'keel' to just being 'hauled'.

In his 1837 novel *Snarleyyow, or the Dog Fiend* Captain Frederick Marryat described a keelhauling, and although a fictional account it tells us much about the actual process. Marryat had entered the Royal Navy in 1806 as a midshipman on Lord Cochrane's frigate *Imperieuse* and had made the rank of captain upon his resignation from the service in 1830. Although he probably never saw a keelhauling first-hand, his account provides an excellent illustration of the procedure:

> *It is nothing more nor less than sending a poor navigator on a voyage of discovery under the bottom of the vessel, lowering him down over the bows, and with ropes retaining him exactly in his position under the kelsom, while he is drawn aft by a hauling line until he makes his appearance at the rudder-chains, generally speaking quite out of breath … because, when so long under the water, he has expended all the breath in his body, and is induced to take in salt water en lieu.*

Marryat was describing the process for keelhauling a man from the bows to the stern on a small, fore-and-aft rigged ship. In larger vessels this would certainly be a death sentence, so unless that was the intended outcome the man would be dragged under the ship from one side to the other. The whole process was compounded by some of the wildlife of the sea. As Marryat relates:

> *In the days of keel-hauling, the bottoms of vessels were not coppered, and in consequence were well studded with a species of shell-fish which attached themselves, called barnacles, and as these shells were all open-mouthed and with sharp cutting points, those who underwent this punishment … were cut and scored all over their body … generally coming up bleeding in every part, and with their faces, especially their noses, as if they had been gnawed by rats.*

In some cases the offender could be weighed down with weights to take him clear of the hull, therefore giving him an extended, and dangerous, ducking. It could be repeated several times until sufficient punishment had been meted out or until the poor unfortunate expired – if that indeed had been the intention.

Keelhauling originated in the Dutch navy of the sixteenth century and was only finally abolished in that navy in the mid-nineteenth century. In the Royal Navy it was not an official punishment and hence not very common; despite this in 1720 the Admiralty decided to formally outlaw the practice. Even in the merchant service it had virtually disappeared by the time Marryat went to sea.

Shanghai

The way this peculiar American saying is used today is a very mild interpretation of the original usage. We might use the word to describe the process of being trapped in a pub by our friends for a period of time longer than envisaged by our partner. In fact 'Shanghai' or 'Shanghaied' specifically means being captured, forced or coerced into a situation or course of action against one's wishes. The other modern use of the word is when 'sourcing' some goods in a not quite legitimate way. For instance in 'The Deep South', a rather watery episode of the TV cartoon comedy *Futurama*, the robot character Bender exclaims, 'Ahoy, mateys. I shanghaied us some hearthy grog'.

In a glorious story that could be the plot for a *film noir*, *The New York Times* of 19 June 1895 declared, 'Wilson was Shanghaied: In his absence his wife was divorced and then married'. This was the bizarre tale of one Jacob Wilson, who claimed he had been 'kept under the influence of liquor for months'. His wife then had him 'shanghaied on board the sailing vessel *Creedmoor*, bound for Australia'. Upon his return Wilson found his wife had divorced him and remarried, defrauding him out of $34,050 in the process.

The use of a geographical place name to describe the process derives from two possible sources. Many of the ships that took on 'shanghaied' men were American vessels operating out of the Western Seaboard ports and destined for Shanghai. Recruitment was a major problem for many American merchant ships so underhand tactics were quite widespread along the Western Seaboard. The men who organised this trade were known as 'crimps', fulfilling the same role as those who worked with the Royal Navy's Impress Service during the age of sail. There were a number of famous crimpers, including the notorious pair in San Francisco, Jim 'Shanghai' Kelly and Johnny 'Shanghai Chicken' Devine. Kelly ran a saloon and boarding house located at 33 Pacific Street, a prime setting for such activities. According to one tall tale Kelly allegedly organised a boat party with free booze to tempt sailors aboard, then delivered the inebriated hands to the captains of three waiting ships. It is this use of the word that forms the plot for the 1915 Charlie Chaplin film *Shanghaied*, where the 'Little Tramp' promises to help a ship owner shanghai some seamen for a voyage.

As well as relating to ships bound for Shanghai, the term could have originated from the local press gangs that operated out of the port of Shanghai in the nineteenth century and who were notoriously effective. Their prey was often American sailors, who, finding themselves ashore in a foreign port would, quite naturally, be tempted by offers of women, drink and drugs. Once suitably inebriated, drugged or distracted, the unfortunate sailor would be clouted over the head and delivered to the captain of an undermanned ship in exchange for a suitable fee.

The process of crimping in American ports was regularly overlooked by notable dignitaries, who occasionally played a part (and took a cut of the fee) in the process. Moreover, the presence of large amounts of labour (as muscle and as votes) was often utilised to gain favourable results in local politics for those who supported crimping. Crimping in the United States was not finally brought to a halt until the twentieth century by two developments. The Seaman's Act of 1915 made crimping a federal offence, while the growing use of steam propulsion in shipping allowed ships to be manned by smaller crews thereby lessening the demand for labour.

Quarantine

To be 'quarantined' is to be detained, perhaps in isolation, for a fixed period of time. This is to allow any signs of disease or illness to appear and, if possible, be treated in that time, thereby (hopefully) preventing the spread of disease. So those in quarantine do not necessarily have a disease, but they have the potential to develop a disease.

In Medieval Europe, towns (especially port towns due to the nature of maritime trade) were rife with contagious diseases. Between 1348 and 1359 the Black Death wiped out about a third of the population of Europe. In response, the town of Dubrovnik, in modern-day Croatia, implemented a system where visitors would spend thirty days on a collection of offshore islands. Any symptoms of the disease would manifest during this time and the people affected would be prevented from entering the city. Shortly after this time the period of detention was extended to forty days. Around the same time the Council of Health at the Italian city of Venice implemented similar measures. The Latin for 'forty days' is *quaranti giornil*, which became anglicised as quarantine. Venice set aside a specific location for the quarantine period – the island of Santa Maria di Nazareth, also giving us the name for the location of a maritime quarantine: a 'lazaretto' or 'lazaret' (the modern name for the island is *Lazaretto Vecchio*).

In Britain the Quarantine Acts of 1710 formalised the practice of quarantining ships returning from overseas locations where plague and disease were known to be prevalent. Initially ships could perform their quarantine before arriving in British waters by spending the required time in lazarets at any number of locations, Malta, Genoa, Marseille or Venice, for example. In home waters a specific location, Stangate Creek, was implemented in the River Medway, but this was for vessels which had either served their quarantine overseas or for ships that did not need to undergo quarantine. From 1800 all ships could serve their quarantine in the Medway, where floating hulks were sometimes utilised to allow the airing of ships stores, contemporary belief being that bad ships' stores were a main source of disease.

As one can imagine, conditions on some quarantined ships could be dreadful. An anonymous account of a passage to Quebec in an Irish emigrant vessel in 1848 described them such: 'In the holds of some of them they said that they were up to their ancles [sic] in filth. The wretched emigrants crowded together like cattle, and corpses remaining long unburied, the sailors being ill, and the passengers unwilling to touch them'.

Because of the belief that disease was spread by the environment rather than human contact, measures undertaken during the time in quarantine were hit and miss. Take the case of the United States brig *Enterprise* which arrived at the New York Quarantine station on 8 July 1822 with ten cases of yellow fever. By 11 July 20 men were sick and all the men were brought ashore so the brig could be whitewashed (even her ballast was whitewashed) cleaned, aired and have her hold 'daily fumigated with nitrous oxide gas'. The men were sent back on board and began to fall ill, then:

Twenty-five days after her arrival, and after repeated whitewashing, letting in water, and constant ventilation one of the sailors obtained permission to take his wife on board: this woman was taken sick on the 9th of August, with yellow fever, after she had been seven days on board, and she died in the Marine Hospital [on Staten Island] on the 18th of that month.

Modern-day methods are more rigorous. For example, in the 2003 outbreak of SARS (Severe Acute Respiratory Syndrome) in Asia, and beyond, those with the disease were kept in isolation and those exposed to the disease but not displaying the symptoms were quarantined. The threat was so great that

President George Bush added SARS to the list of diseases the US deems as necessitating quarantine measures.

Not enough room to swing a cat

This phrase habitually crops up in modern day usage, perhaps leaving the uninitiated reaching for the telephone to call the Royal Society for the Prevention of Cruelty to Animals with frantic tales of people swinging cats around by their tails. Of course, this phrase has nothing to do with maniacal moggie manoeuvres. It is often used to describe a small space, perhaps a cramped basement flat or an en-suite 'bathroom' in a bed and breakfast.

Take this typical nugget from the king of the quip, Groucho Marx in the 1931 film *Monkey Business*: 'If this is the Captain, I'm gonna have a few words with him. My hot water's been cold for three days. And I haven't got room enough in here to swing a cat. In fact, I haven't even got a cat'. Another example can be provided by Mark Twain's *Roughing It*, where the main character is bound for Hawaii on board the tiny ship *Boomerang*:

> *The little low-ceiled cabin below was rather larger than a hearse, and as dark as a vault. It had two coffins on each side—I mean two bunks. A small table, capable of accommodating three persons at dinner, stood against the forward bulkhead, and over it hung the dingiest whale oil lantern that ever peopled the obscurity of a dungeon with ghostly shapes. The floor room unoccupied was not extensive. One might swing a cat in it, perhaps, but not a long cat.*

The naval origin is more sinister than using a cat as a makeshift measuring device. When a seaman was to be flogged for a crime, the actual punishment would always be carried out on deck. This was because in Nelson's time the 'cat' was the cat-o'-nine-tails, an impressive lash which measured about 4 feet (2 feet for the rope handle and 2 feet for the tails). The space between decks on a warship was often quite small and cramped. For instance, while in command of HMS *Speedy*, admittedly a small ship, Lord Cochrane recalled, '… my only practicable mode of shaving consisted in removing the skylight, and putting my head through to make a toilet table of the quarter deck.' Even on a large ship-of-the-line the room between decks was rather cramped. So the only place a cat could be swung with the force required in punishment was on deck, as below decks there was, literally, not enough room to swing a cat.

The cat-o'-nine-tails was the instrument of punishment in floggings. Smyth describes it thus, '... commonly of nine pieces of line or cord, about half a yard long, fixed upon a piece of thick rope for a handle, and having three knots on each, at small intervals, nearest one end'. He then rather laconically adds, 'with this the seamen who transgresses are flogged upon the bare back'.

The parallel lacerations upon the man's back would be similar to those inflicted by a cat scratch, hence it's name. Due to the fact that the captain of a ship could only order a flogging it was also known as the 'captain's daughter'. A variation of the cat was known as the 'thieves' cat', which was only used to punish the crime of theft, the cat had additional knots tied in it to compound the injuries inflicted during the flogging.

In well run ships floggings were not that common and a new cat would be made for each dose of punishment, either by a Bosun's mate or the man about to be punished. It would be kept in a red or blue baize bag until the appointed time. Lashes were usually given in dozens and could range from a single dozen right into the hundreds. The whole act of assembling the men on deck and the rituals associated with the punishment gave the whole experience a quasi religious element, all of which was designed to increase the visual effect of witnessing the flogging, and therefore, hopefully, dissuading the assembled mariners from future transgressions. Flogging was abolished in the United States Navy in 1850 and the Royal Navy in 1879.

Perhaps we should leave the last word on capital punishment to a hero of naval fiction. C.S. Forester's Captain Horatio Hornblower must have spoken for many real and enlightened officers when he stated, 'Flogging only makes a bad man worse ... but it can break a good man's spirit'.

6

MUNJY

A sailor's life involved lots of manual labour, hauling on ropes, climbing up the rigging, rowing, stoking coal, shifting munitions and so on; hence food was the fuel that allowed a man-of-war to function. But food can be more than just nutrition; it can also be a source of comfort, a constant in an unpredictable environment. From Greek and Roman times to the men who crew the nuclear submarines of today, food has been a basic necessity. As the great administrator of the Stuart Navy Samuel Pepys recognised:

> *Englishmen, and more especially seamen, love their bellies above anything else, and therefore it must always be remembered in the management of the victualling of the Navy that to make any abatement from them in the quantity or agreeableness of the victuals is to discourage and provoke them in the tenderest point and will sooner render them disgusted with the King's service than any one other hardship that can be put upon them.*

As a result the sailor's relationship with their food was, and remains, a key consideration. The sailor's day was organised around mealtimes; breakfast around 08:00, the main meal, called dinner, was served in the middle of the day, usually at 12 noon, sometimes a tea at 16:00 and then supper at 19:00.

The ideal sailor's diet would contain plenty of fresh meat, vegetables and fruit, but for many years this was rarely achievable at sea. The quality of fresh produce can decline rapidly; this led to all sorts of procedures to prolong the life of food.

Meat was preserved with salt and stowed in barrels, this, combined with the spartan cooking facilities on board ship and the nature of the messing system, limited the type of dishes available. Meals that were hearty, warming and easy to cook, such as stews, were popular with the sailors.

In the Royal Navy of the eighteenth and nineteenth centuries food came from two sources: official supplies from Admiralty contractors and victualling yards and locally sourced supplies paid for by the purser of the ship acting under the guidance of the captain. Sailors were fed a diet adequate for the needs of their work, and on occasion better than they could expect on land. Malnourishment was not an issue; it would have left the seamen unable to fulfil their duties. The real threat was scurvy, but by Nelson's time the British Admiralty had implemented several measures to combat this debilitating disease, most importantly the regular supply of fresh limes and lemons to ships. During the wars with France ships blockading French naval bases were re-supplied at sea. During the nineteenth century tinned food helped solve many of the problems of food preservation, even if it produced some interesting slang terms for the contents of the tins!

For a sailor in Nelson's navy, the weekly ration was set down as:

7 lb ship's biscuit
4 lb beef
2 lb pork
2 pints of peas
3 pints of oatmeal
6 oz butter
12 oz cheese

To which, of course, would be added drink (see Chapter 7).

By the time of the First World War, despite the advances in food preservation, the diet in the Royal Navy had not changed that much. In 1914 the daily ration was:

½ lb meat, including the bone
1 lb potatoes
1 oz milk
1 oz tea
Small amounts of sugar, salt, etc.

Each mess was also allocated four pence per day to buy extras, for example soup powder, tomatoes, bacon, cheese, bloater paste, which were purchased from the canteen using 'mess chits'. As well as availability, there were variations according to nationality; pasta on Italian ships, rice on Japanese and some Russian ships even had caviar.

The twentieth century saw a new problem for naval administrators to tackle; the submarine. Food lasted an even shorter time in the dark, damp and cramped boats. Bread would spoil within days and other fresh foodstuffs would soon be used up leaving the ubiquitous tinned food: meat, fish, milk and cheese alongside powdered foods such as eggs. The very nature of living a submerged lifestyle caused its own health issues and so compensation sometimes came in the form of extra food. Robert Lagane of the French Navy recalled:

> *The quality of the grub was one of the attractions of a career in submarines. The regulations laid down 'a protein-rich diet accompanied by milk rations', in order to prevent any risk of anaemia caused by the lead in the batteries and by carbon dioxide. These two measures meant a doubling or even tripling of the standard food allowance ... One of my first surprises was to hear that every order involving a change of activity was immediately followed by an order to have a snack.*

Cooking, if it could be called that, could only be done when surfaced; when submerged, cold rations were the norm.

So what does the modern sailor eat? The British Ministry of Defence allowed the captain and crew of HMS *Sceptre* (a *Swiftsure* class submarine launched in 1978) to publish a mouth-watering sample weekend menu on the Royal Navy's website: www.royal-navy.mod.uk.

Friday

Breakfast
Cereals, grilled bacon, grilled sausage, eggs to order, baked beans,
plum tomatoes, orange juice, black pudding & toast

Lunch
Battered haddock with lemon/Poached cod du glare/Cheeseburger
Chips & mushy peas

Dinner
Chicken Satay with Tagliatelli/London roast/vegetarian to order
Medley of vegetables/boiled potatoes
Jam sponge & custard

Saturday

Breakfast
As for Friday but with the addition of sautéed mushrooms

Lunch
Potato bar – assorted fillings: raviolli, beans, curried chicken,
cheese, tuna, coleslaw

Dinner
Grilled fillet steak/scampi tartare/vegetarian to order
Pont neuf potatoes/mushrooms/onions/grilled tomatoes/sweetcorn
Cheese & biscuits

Sunday

Breakfast
As for Friday and Saturday, but with the addition of grapefruit segments
Lunch
Roast beef & yorkshire pudding/roast chicken & stuffing/vegetarian to order
Roast potatoes/boiled potatoes/carrots/
cauliflower mornay & rich brown gravy
Fruit trifle and cream
Dinner
Pizza – margherita, meatfeast, pepperoni, Hawaiian
Garlic bread, chips & beans

As with most things, the sailor took all the interesting problems thrown at him in his stride; his inventive mind coming up with a host of slang terms for various foodstuffs.

Sweet Fanny Adams

This is an interesting phrase, often used colloquially in place of a rather more colourful phrase, 'Sweet F*** All', to mean 'absolutely nothing' or 'completely useless'. As the journalist Yvonne Roberts pontificated in *The Guardian* newspaper in March 2008, 'Codes of practice and "self-regulation" have done sweet fanny adams to stop relentless advertising to children'. In polite society it is regarded as quite proper to shorten the phrase to '**Sweet F.A**'. It is possibly that many people who use the phrase today don't realise the tragic story behind its origin and how the British sailor, with his own unique sense of black humour, added a twist to the tale.

Fanny Adams was an 8-year-old Hampshire girl. Just after lunchtime on Saturday, 24 August 1867, a fine sunny day, she went for a walk with her sister Lizzie and a friend Millie Warner. In the narrow country lanes near their home of Alton they bumped into solicitor's clerk Frederick Baker. He offered Lizzie and Millie a silver three halfpence coin to go off and spend and Fanny a halfpenny to join him on a walk along the lane. Fanny accepted the coin, but refused to go with Baker. He promptly picked her up and made off into a nearby hop field. Lizzie and Millie headed home and raised the alarm. Despite bumping into Baker, who maintained that he gave the children the money to buy sweets, Fanny's mother could not find her missing daughter. It was not until evening that neighbours, searching the fields, made a shocking and grisly discovery. Fanny's body was found, her head and legs cut off, her eyes torn out and her guts and organs thrown around the hop field.

Baker was quickly arrested. His shirt and trousers had suspicious bloodstains and he had two knives on him. Witnesses placed him in the area at the time of Fanny's disappearance. Later investigations turned up a chilling confession in Baker's diary for that day, 'killed a young girl'. In fact Baker, who had apparently been drinking and whose family had a history of mental health problems combined with violence, had beaten her brains out with a stone before embarking upon his frenzied desecration of the corpse. Unsurprisingly, Baker was found guilty of the murder after just fifteen minutes deliberation by a jury at Winchester County Assizes and hanged on Christmas Eve 1867. Fanny was buried in the churchyard at Alton Cemetery, where her grave can still be seen.

The story, as brutal and sensational as it was, might have ended there, but for the Admiralty. Two years after the murder the Royal Navy started issuing mutton in tins as rations for its seamen. The initial response was not good; in fact the sailors were so displeased with the new victuals that they mused whether the dubious meat was in fact the body parts of the dismembered girl. Hence, in the Royal Navy tinned meat was known as 'sweet Fanny Adams', sweet because of the tender age of the girl. As the actual tins used to case the meat could also be converted into mess tins, these were then referred to as a 'fanny'. The fact that the sailors thought the meat completely useless led to the phrase going ashore and being used in a similar way. As to whether this had any influence on the British 1970s' four-piece The Sweet's decision to entitle their 1974 album *Sweet Fanny Adams*, only those with more than a passing interest in glam rock will be able to answer.

Chewing the fat

Today when people want to mull over a problem or a situation they might say they are off to 'chew the fat' with a friend or colleague. What they mean is that they are going to have a good-natured, informal discussion; to mull

it over or to seek counsel. As Franky Four Fingers, the jewel thief in Guy Ritchie's mockney gangster caper *Snatch* (2000) remarks, 'I have stones to sell, fat to chew, and many different men to see about many different dogs, so if I am not rushing you'.

As one might suspect, the nautical origin of this phrase does relate to food. On the warships of many nations the **hands** were allowed to choose who they messed with (six men being a usual number) – they would take their food together at a mess table. While seated and chewing through their, perhaps rather fatty, rations they would share gossip, share news or just grumble. We have already seen what Royal Navy sailors thought about their tinned mutton, but that was not the only type of ration that drew negative comments. Sailors often complained about the quality of most of their food, especially towards the end of a long voyage when all the decent provisions had long gone. A particular culprit was salt beef, a tough meat, cured to ensure it would not rot away on long voyages, and which required a lot of mastication to make it swallowable.

Chow

Chow is a word often used for food, especially in English-speaking countries and is a particular favourite of United States service personnel. Take this quote from Hawkeye in the classic US comedy programme M*A*S*H:

I think I'm getting delirious. I'm just having warm, friendly thoughts about the gourmet leftovers at the 4077 chow line.

Ashore there must be many people who walk into Chinese restaurants and take-aways and order the dish of chow-mein but fail to put two and two together. 'Chow' is derived from the Chinese dish of *chow-chow*, a mixture of cold pickles usually consisting of cabbage, carrots, asparagus, beans and cauliflower. As '*mein*' is the Chinese Han character meaning 'noodles', *chow-mein* is vegetable noodles. Moreover, the term 'chow-chow' was shortened in Pidgin English to just plain 'chow' by the Chinese when that country was opened up to Western trade in the nineteenth century. Having a standardised word for food would certainly have helped bewildered American sailors when faced with the complex pronunciation problems of Cantonese, never mind the completely alien nature of the written character script.

In the southern United States there is a version of chow-chow relish that derived from the French word *chou*, cabbage, although it is likely that the Chinese source predates this usage. Finally, knowing the black humour prevalent in sailors of all nations regarding the possible sources of their food, it cannot have failed to escape the notice of nineteenth-century wags that a chow-chow is also the English name for a Chinese breed of dog. As well as claiming to be one of the oldest breeds of dog in the world, a 2003 study found them to be also one of the most stupid. This is not surprising as Stanley Coren, author of *The Intelligence of Dogs*, remarked, 'Chows were originally bred as food animals. Who needs smart food?' Though chow, meaning food, did not come from eating the chow dog. The dog was called a chow because when they were imported into Britain, Coren argues, they were classified as 'miscellaneous merchandise' and the crates containing them were marked with the Pidgin English: 'chow-chow'. In some areas of China they are still bred for food, culinary connoisseurs amongst you take note: apparently black dogs taste better fried, other colours are more appropriate for stewing – so perhaps the sailors were not too far off the mark!

Slush fund

This is one of those great nautical phrases that so many people use today without any idea where it comes from. A 'slush fund' usually consists of a little cash, either in petty cash or as savings, put aside. This could be for many uses, though the original concept was to spend the money on little luxuries. The money could also serve as a reserve for a 'rainy day'. In government and big business a 'slush fund' has slightly darker connotations: it usually refers to money secretly put aside using some underhand or even illegal methods, i.e. the money remains out of sight of the general public and is usually kept off the public accounts.

In the political sphere such money can be used as extra funds with which to fight elections, thereby circumventing the usual methods of raising, spending and auditing of campaign contributions. In 1952 Richard Nixon's election as running mate to Dwight Eisenhower's presidential campaign was the subject of severe criticism. Many publications including the *New York Post* claimed that Nixon had created a personal 'slush fund' to help him win the contest. The scheme involved several Californian millionaires contributing to a fund to supplement Nixon's income as a senator, thereby giving him increased spending power in the vice-president ticket. When the allegations came to light Nixon took to television to defend himself; in fact, so effective was his so called 'Checkers Speech' that it created a wave of support and thereby helped Eisenhower into the White House.

Two decades later Nixon was at it again: during the Watergate scandal a slush fund based in Mexico was found to have been created to fund a series of illegal activities, including break-ins, wiretapping, espionage and other shenanigans, even providing 'hush money' to those caught breaking into the Democratic National Committee headquarters at the Watergate hotel complex in Washington on 17 June 1972. Nixon was caught out and forced to resign, the only US President to date to suffer this ultimate humiliation.

What was the original slush fund? When meat is boiled the fat tends to separate from the flesh. On board ship, when the cook had prepared, cooked and served up the usually heavily salted meat, the fatty residue left behind in the ships cauldrons (known as coppers) was certainly not allowed to go to waste. In fact, it was one of the perks of the ship's cook to be allowed to collect the fat and then sell it on, usually to the ship's purser when at sea. This gave the cook (who was usually an older and sometimes disabled ex-seaman employed on a sinecure) a bit of extra cash. The purser would, in turn, use the fat to make candles for sale to the crew. There were other uses for the left over fat: mixed with linseed oil and tallow it could be used to grease ropes thereby allowing them to run smoothly and giving them a longer lifespan by providing a waterproof covering. This perhaps gave the term widespread use ashore as a slush fund allows certain palms to be 'greased' thereby ensuring favourable outcomes.

Peter Jeans points to the possible Norwegian source of the word – perhaps coming from the word *sluss* meaning 'mud' or 'mire', while some sources suggest other Scandinavian words, *slask* meaning 'slushy ground' or the Danish for sleet *slus* or *sluske*. It is no surprise that these words became associated with cooking as thawing snow and sleet have an appearance similar to separated meat fat. Moreover, the fact that slush (both fat and snow) is soft and a bit wet is probably the reason why many people call over-the-top sentimental novels and films 'slushy' (as it also seems they are designed to make their primarily female audience 'blubber' away).

Piping hot

> *'Now, my boy, I hope you're good and hungry, because breakfast will be ready as soon as the sun's up, and we'll have a piping hot one, too.'*
> The Adventures of Tom Sawyer by Mark Twain

The method of cooking and distributing food on board ship seems a little chaotic to twenty-first-century minds. Men were divided into messes and each mess would appoint a representative responsible for collecting the daily rations, depositing them with the cook, and then collecting the prepared food from the galley. But after the ship's cook had done his worst to produce a meal for the crew, there remained one problem. On small ships it was easy to know when food was ready, sailors would be able to smell and hear food being prepared. On large ships, where a man might be working aloft or down in the hold, how were they to know that it was dinner time? The Boatswain's pipe was used to call the crew. It had a high pitch and could be heard above all the other background noise aboard ship, so when the Boatswain piped for dinner the crew knew that the food was ready to be served. The food was therefore 'piping hot'.

A square meal

> *'Grandpa! How can you act like that? After all Herman has done for you. Why, if it wasn't for him, you'd still be back in the old country, hanging around in some damp old cave, scratching fleas out of your wings and wondering who your next square meal was coming from!'*
> Lily Munster, The Munsters

In modern-day usage a 'square meal' is one that is satisfying and nutritious. It is a stock term for many writers of literature, films and television scripts. Take this example from Edwin Cole's 1948 *John Studebaker, an American Dream*: 'the sign outside read, unfortunately, "Square meals $3.00 each. Pay in advance." The vision of a square meal made their mouths water.' Or even before that Mark Twain's 1889 *A Connecticut Yankee in King Arthur's Court*: 'My presence gave the monks hope, and cheered them up a good deal; insomuch that they ate a square meal that night for the first time in ten days'.

Sailors required a calorie-rich diet to be able to perform their duties, and would be fed three times a day: breakfast, dinner and supper. Naval issue plates were square, and possibly give us the term 'square meal'. HMS *Invincible* was a former French ship captured at the First Battle of Finisterre in 1747 and incorporated into the Royal Navy. On Sunday, 19 February 1758, she hit the Horse Tail sandbank in the Solent and began taking in water. Despite the best efforts of the crew she remained stuck fast on the sandbank. All her cargo and cannon were taken off before, on the 22nd, she went over and sank. In May 1979 a local fisherman, Arthur Mack, found the wreck. Divers investigating the site found a number of square wooden plates which the sailors would have used; they are now on display at the Historic Dockyard, Chatham.

It is commonly presumed that sailors' plates were made of wooden squares for a number of reasons: wood was cheap and it would not break, unlike pottery; square shapes stow easier than round ones; they would move around less in bad weather and so be easier to eat from; and they could be easily made by the ship's carpenter. Each of the plates found in the *Invincible* had raised edges. This was most likely to keep food on the plate, but also to provide a degree of regularity in dishing out portions in each mess. The raised edges were called 'fiddles', which made it easy to spot any sailor taking more than his share of food. This possibly gave rise to another commonly used phrase: 'on the fiddle'. If the portion touched the sides, i.e. was literally touching or 'on the fiddle' then that sailor had too much, which was a punishable offence.

It is also thought in some circles that the use of the square plate also gave rise to '**three square meals a day**'.

There is, however, some debate as to whether 'square' refers to the shape of the plate or another meaning of square: a fair deal. It could have the same origin as the phrases 'square deal' and 'fair and square'. Therefore a 'square meal' would be one that is a suitable portion of food for the money exchanged, for instance, from the *Harpers New Monthly Magazine* of 1865: 'For fifty cents you CAN GET A GOOD SQUARE MEAL at the HOWLING WILDERNESS SALOON!' For that princely sum the hungry diner would receive 'a substantial repast of pork and beans, onions, cabbage, and other articles of sustenance'.

Despite 'square meal' being a favourite phrase of mariners and landlubbers all over the world we will probably never know the true origin. All we know is that it has widespread use, as midshipman Douglas King-Harman, of HMS *Lord Nelson*, explained to his father in 1909: 'I am the Midshipman of the Picket Boat, so that I don't get much time to myself. In fact I can't fit in a square meal edgeways. Just as I sit down simply ravening, then it's 'Away Picket Boat', and away I dash'.

Hardtack

The word tack is usually associated with the course of a sailing a ship but in this instance tack does not relate to a sailing term but instead to ship's biscuit. This was a rather interesting concoction designed to solve one of the great seafaring problems, namely to create a nutritious foodstuff that would not spoil on long voyages and to be easy to store. The answer was a flour-based baked biscuit, known to the world as 'ship's biscuit'.

The biscuit formed the hardy staple of the sailor's diet until the introduction of tinned foodstuffs in the nineteenth century. Even after this date, the biscuit was still issued as part of rations. During the time of the Spanish Armada, English sailors were supposed to receive a daily allowance of 1lb of ship's biscuit. Visitors to the National Maritime

Museum, Greenwich, in London can see a later example that bears the inscription, 'This biscuit was given – Miss Blacket at Berwick on Tuesday 13 April 1784, Berwick'. Biscuits for the Royal Navy were mass-produced ashore at special baking houses in the Royal Navy Victualling Yards. The bakehouse at Plymouth could manufacture enough biscuits every day to feed 16,000 men.

Due to the coarse and very hard nature of the biscuit it was known as 'hardtack', as opposed to 'softtack', which was more like traditional bread and was freshly baked onboard ship. Frequently the biscuit was so hard it posed a danger to sailors' teeth, so they would usually soak it in some kind of fluid to soften it up and make it more palatable; sometimes with coffee for breakfast or with water, soup or even beer. If no liquid was available then the biscuit could, albeit with some difficulty, be broken into smaller pieces. In the United States Navy ship's biscuits were nicknamed 'monitors' after the first ironclad warship commissioned into the Federal navy.

Alongside dental dangers, the biscuit could also attract pests in the form of weevils – small burrowing beetles that would make the hardtack their home and then lay their larvae. One way to get rid of them was to bang the biscuit against the mess table, thereby sending the weevils tumbling out. During the American Civil War soldiers would drop their hardtack into coffee, the weevils would float to the surface allowing the soldier to scoop them out and resume his meal. Writing in 1904 one young naval cadet told his mother, 'At 8:45 we have a glass of ripping milk & weevily dog biscuits, the only article of fare that is not splendid'. So, the word 'hardtack' became known to the wider world to refer to poor quality food that does not live up to expectation.

Should any reader be crazy enough to try making their own, here is a recipe for the ship's biscuit courtesy of the Royal Naval Museum:

Plain ship's biscuit
Add water to 1lb medium coarse stone-ground wholemeal flour and ¼oz salt to make a stiff dough. Leave for 30 minutes and then roll out very thickly. Separate into 5 or 7 biscuits. Bake in a hot oven approx. 420°F for 30 minutes. Leave biscuits in a warm, dry atmosphere to harden and dry out.

Lobscouse

> *'Mr Martin,' said Jack, after the chaplain had said grace, 'it occurred to me that perhaps you might not yet have seen lobscouse.'*
>
> The Far Side of the World by Patrick O'Brian

This is one of those bizarre words that landlubbers have little knowledge of in its full form, but part of the word is famous the world over. *Lapskaus* is a stewed Norwegian dish, traditionally consisting of mutton or beef (or even corned beef), potatoes, vegetables (primarily carrots) and **hardtack** (see above) broken up and dropped in. In Norway, where it is so popular it could be considered the national dish, it was made with meat and vegetables left over from the weekend (similar to the English bubble and squeak). This simple, yet hearty stew made it a firm favourite with Norwegian sailors who were responsible for spreading it round the world. In Brooklyn, New York, Eighth Avenue was known colloquially as Lapskaus Avenue due to the large immigrant Norwegian population.

But it is in the north west of England, and in particular Liverpool, that the dish can be said to have had the greatest influence. Even today many Liverpool pubs and cafés still have the dish on their menus as Lob Scows, or even Lobscouse. It is this latter word that has given the world 'Scouse' – the slang term for anyone from Liverpool. The Scouse accent is distinctly different to other regional accents and is a product of the melting pot that the port of Liverpool became during the nineteenth century. As well as generations of Welsh, Scots and Irish immigrants into the city, influences from many other corners of the globe were added in. At one time Liverpool was a major trading partner of many Scandinavian ports, perhaps this is where Liverpudlian sailors started to acquire a taste for *Lapskaus*, which they would have brought back with them and which is still enjoyed today.

Limey

> *'Lois, the bar has been taken over by a bunch of lousy, limey, no-good, tea-sucking British bastards.'*
> Peter Griffin, *Family Guy*

This is a common insult thrown at British people (and the English in particular) by Americans.

The origins of the insult come from the 'scurvy problem'. One of the constant difficulties for navies in the age of sail was the provision of fresh fruit and vegetables. An absence of such led to the disease scurvy, which is caused by a deficiency in ascorbic acid contained in vitamin C. Just about everyone who went to sea during these times suffered from the disease at one time or another.

Symptoms include:
Bleeding and soft gums, often leading to tooth loss
Bleeding from all mucous membranes (mouth, eyes, nose)
Sunken eyes
Opening of previously healed scars
Separation of healed bone fractures

In some cases it was very mild and cleared up when fresh provisions were sourced, but if not treated scurvy would prove fatal. It is a pertinent fact that more sailors usually died from disease than enemy action. When Commodore George Anson returned to England in 1744 after a four-year circumnavigation of the globe there were only 500 survivors of the original complement of 1900 men who had set sail. The overwhelming cause of death was disease or starvation, with scurvy figuring prominently amongst the fatalities.

Although the cause of the disease and some of the preventative measures were known in the early 1600s the precise nature of the disease was not understood until 1747 when the Scotsman James Lind, a former ship's surgeon, experimented with various cures on a dozen scorbutic (having scurvy) sailors. His results were striking. Most of the sailors were still suffering except two who received supplements of oranges and lemons; one had recovered enough to be considered fit for duty and the other was not too far behind. Despite the success, Lind's findings were overlooked. It was not until 1794 that the Scottish physician Sir Gilbert Blane instructed that men onboard the *Suffolk*, off on a voyage to India, were to have lime juice mixed with their daily grog tot. This prevented any serious scurvy problems. Faced with this evidence, the following year the Admiralty acted and issued lemon juice to the entire Royal Navy.

But why 'limey', and not 'lemony' or 'orangey'? In the British Caribbean colonies, which had an extensive trade with the Eastern American Seaboard, the lime was more common, so this source of vitamin C that was issued to Royal Navy ship and British Merchantmen. Hence Americans called them 'lime-juicers' which was quickly shortened to 'limeys'.

Munjy

'Munjy', as the chapter heading suggests, is the sailors' traditional slang name for food. Possible origins are the French *manger*, with an alternative being from *mangiare*' the Italian for 'to eat'. There are so many slang phrases that sailors have used for various foodstuffs that it is impossible to list them all in a work of this nature. Some you will find ashore, and they perhaps even started ashore before being taken to sea by sailors. Others started at sea. Some of them are self-explanatory, some are not, and some are downright disgusting. Below is a menu to give the reader a flavour of the sailor's diet and unique mindset.

--- ❖ ---

Breakfast Menu

Dartmoor mutiny
*Porridge, the poor quality of which allegedly caused
unrest at Dartmoor Prison in 1932.*

Monkey dicks
Chipolata sausages

Snorkers
*As recommended by Lieutenant James Bennett
in Monsarrat's **The Cruel Sea**, snorkers are sausages, specifically
Henry Palethorpe's pre-cooked tinned sausages.*

Cackleberrys
Eggs, specifically lovely boiled eggs

Spithead pheasant/One-eyed steak
Kippers (sometimes served with a poached egg)

Yellow peril
Smoked Haddock

Tram smash
*Bacon and arigonies (tinned tomato) – sometimes
including dried scrambled egg*

Chicken on a raft
Egg served on (sometimes deep fried) toast

--- ❖ ---

Dinner Menu

Elephant's footprints served on a red lead jus
Spam fritters with tinned tomatoes

Schooner on the rocks
Roast shin of beef served upon a bed of roast potatoes

Babies' heads in jippers
Tinned steak and kidney pudding in gravy

Three-decker topped with clakker
Three layers of meat and dough, topped off with a pie crust

Acting rabbit
Meat pie baked in the oven

Floaters in the snow
Sausages served on mashed potatoes

Dessert Menu

Chinese wedding cake
Rice pudding with gammies (currants or raisins)

Figgy duff and thickers
*Steamed suet pudding (usually containing fruit,
though not necessarily figs) served with condensed milk*

Bathing beauty
*Blancmange, so called because it shivers
and has lovely curves!*

Black-coated workers served with oojah
Stewed prunes with custard

Depth charges
*Stewed figs, no further explanation of the
origins of this one necessary!*

Pipes/tubes
Macaroni pudding

———◆———

Supper Menu

Cheesy 'ammy eggy
*Toast covered in cheese with bacon or ham & topped
with a fried or poached egg*

BITS/Windy beans/Haricots musicales
Baked Beans in tomato sauce

HITS
Herrings in tomato sauce

Shit on a raft
Devilled kidneys on toast

Cheese oosh
*Omelette made with reconstituted egg and milk,
sometimes covered with tinned baked beans*

Assorted nutty
Chocolate, whether or not it contains nuts, and other sweets

Pozzie and soft tack
Jam or marmalade & bread

———◆———

(Please see Chapter 7 – Grog – for the drinks.)

7

GROG

Alongside food and women, the sailor's thoughts were (and to a degree still are) dominated by drink; not just alcoholic drinks, though they did make up a very large part of the sailor's diet. The importance of the scuttlebutt as a source of refreshing drinking water has been discussed in Chapter 4, but many a sailor has sought comfort in the warming properties of tea, coffee and hot chocolate. This is extremely pertinent on modern ships of the United States Navy, which are dry, i.e. they carry no alcoholic drinks.

The story starts with beer. Long before rum became associated with British sailors, beer was the drink on board ship. In fact, beer was part of the sailor's daily ration. Nelson's sailors received 1 gallon per day, approximately eight pints. Sailors almost demanded it by right, until the daily ration was abolished in 1831. In 1805 one George Mason received 300 lashes for refusing to obey an order because, 'it was a damn shame he could not get any beer'. It was more important than water; due to the alcohol content, beer would keep for longer at sea than water. As the beer was often quite weak, and as water is the main ingredient in beer, the sailors would receive most of their daily intake of fluid through drinking it. Strong beer, like porters or stouts (7–8% volume), kept well, but the penny-pinching brewers often supplied inferior beer, generally known as 'small beer' or 'sea beer', which contained considerably less alcohol. The calorific content of beer was also an important part of the sailor's daily energy intake.

In home waters beer was readily available, being produced in royal breweries. In 1525 Portsmouth alone had five, producing huge quantities for the fleet: 100 tuns a day, i.e. around 100,000 litres (1 tun is equivalent to approximately 252 gallons or 954 litres). Due to the ever-increasing demand some of the brewers cut corners, but beer produced by brewing too quickly would not last long. At least this was what the book *Advice of a Seaman* suggested when it appeared in 1634:

> *The brewers have gotten the art to sophisticate beer with broom instead of hops, and ashes instead of malt, and (to make it more lively) to pickle it with salt water so that, whilst it is new, it shall seemingly be worthy of praise, but in one month was worse than stinking water.*

Overseas, once the beer casks were emptied, locally produced drinks would be substituted in the ratio of a pint of wine, or half pint of brandy, rum or arrack per gallon of beer. These beverages, even when diluted into grog, could produce raucous behaviour among the sailors not used to strong liquor. Surgeon Leonard Gillespie of the *Racehorse* wrote on 16 January 1788, 'Grog was this day issued to the seamen, the beer being expended and as is pretty usual attended with some riotousness'. Despite this wine, or grog, was usually issued to the sailors at 11:30 in the morning, i.e. before dinner, and at four o'clock in the afternoon, though not all ships served it every day. Selling or trading of this ration amongst members of the ship's company was strictly forbidden, 'the consequences of which prove too often fatal, from accidents as well as creating disease owing to drunkenness'. The problems associated with alcohol excess are borne out on the 'Black List' (see Chapter 5) of HMS *Drake* for 1811–12 where the majority of crimes were 'drunkenness' or 'repeated drunkenness', or offences that could possibly be drink related such as 'insolence', 'skulking', 'neglect of duty', 'fighting' and the unsociable 'drunkenness and pissing in his hammock'. The rum 'tot' (named after the Old English for small child, 'tot'; the ration being smaller than the beer ration) was finally abolished on 31 July 1970 also known as 'The Black Day'.

If beer and grog were the preserve of the men, the drink of choice for officers was wine. Generally, as long as an officer could keep sober on watch his superiors would turn a blind eye to alcohol consumption. On HMS *Monarch* in 1756 a mess of four warrant officers were polishing off two gallons a day. On board HMS *Argo* in 1761 Captain Clements had collected this phenomenal list of booze:

Messina: 1 butt, 3 kegs of 40 gallons each
Port: 2 hogsheads
Cyprus: 2 kegs, 1 demijohn, 2 bottles
Champagne: 6 dozen bottles
Burgundy: 12 dozen bottles
Claret: 12 dozen and 7 bottles
Frontenac: 6 bottles
Montepulciano: 1 chest
Florence: 8½ chests
Malvasia: 2 chests
Rum: 1 dozen and nine bottles
Beer: 3 dozen and 6 bottles
Source: N.A.M. Rodger, *The Wooden World*

It should be pointed out that consumption of alcohol was also widespread ashore during the age of sail. Miscreants on board prison hulks stationed in the River Thames were provided with two pints of beer for four days of the week. It was also common practice to allow children to drink beer at breakfast time. Drinking alcohol was an accepted part of everyday life.

If there were difficulties obtaining booze, then the sailor turned his inventive mind to the solution. During the Siege of Malta in the Second World War many things were in short supply but on board one HM Submarine operating out of the island, Torpedo Gunner's Mate J. C. Brighton discovered a couple of men 'behaving in a strange manner. Their eyes were glazed, their speech was slurred and they smelt strongly of liquor'. Knowing that they could not have been storing up their rum ration, Brighton decided to investigate the torpedo tube room which he found to be 'dark and evil-smelling'. The reason was 'a pair of pants or a vest containing some kind of sloppy mush, with a tin underneath to catch the liquor as it percolated through. Sadly, I had to commit this concoction to the gash bucket, without even a taste'. What he had found was Pumpkin rum – sailors would open up a large pumpkin, remove the pulp and stuff the inside with brown sugar. Left to mature in a muslin bag it produced liquor.

It should also be remembered that the traditions of sailing transgressed national borders. Kurt Guennel on board the German U-boat *U-95* remarked of her departure from a French harbour in 1941: 'The evening before there had been the usual goodbye parties, which usually end in the majority of the men becoming helplessly drunk'.

The important role that drinking has played across the centuries in the daily life on the sailor has invariably led to him assigning numerous slang terms for drinks, drinking rituals and the sometimes less than pleasant consequences of drunkenness.

Grog

Tis grog, only grog,
Is his rudder, his compass, his cable, his log;
The sailor's sheet-anchor is grog
From 'The Sailor's Sheet Anchor is Grog' (the sheet anchor was usually unused and kept in reserve)

The full version of this nineteenth-century ditty lampooning the life of a sailor poses some interesting questions: how did he cope with the dangers inherent in his profession? What happened if his friend scarpered with his prize money or if his girl sought comforts from another? The answer was simple; he turned to drink. Grog in particular.

Mention the word 'grog' and anyone with even just a passing interest in nautical affairs will know what you are talking about. Moreover, thanks to the plethora of pirate-related books and films, most people who have never even seen the sea let alone boarded a ship will also think they know what grog is.

However, despite it being used as such by Antipodeans, grog is not just any type of booze and it's certainly not beer. Grog is a rum-based drink. Rum first served to British sailors in the West Indies, but not by Admiral Edward 'Old Grogram' Vernon, as is commonly believed. Instead it was Vice Admiral William Penn's fleet, sent out by Oliver Cromwell and which captured Jamaica in 1655, that ran out of beer and first issued rum to British sailors. Although alcoholic drink in the form of beer was an important part of the sailor's diet and they would be accustomed to alcohol consumption the effects of serving spirits neat to the men was disastrous: it caused all sorts of problems both on ship and ashore, drunkenness led to fights, accidents and death.

It was not until August 1740 that Admiral Vernon decided to solve these problems by officially sanctioning the crew's 'half pint of rum to be daily mixed with a quart of water'. In order to show the men that there was no scrimping on their rum ration Vernon gave precise instructions that the mixing was to take place in a **scuttlebutt** on deck 'in the presence of the Lieutenant of the Watch, who is to take particular care to see that the men are not defrauded in having their full allowance of rum'. The resulting grog was to be issued in two servings 'between the hours of 10 and 12 in the morning, and the other between 4 and 6 in the afternoon'. In order to make the drink a bit tastier, Vernon encouraged that sugar and limes should be added. As well as preventing the worst excesses of drunkenness, serving the rum in this way prevented sailors from storing up neat rum for a an illicit 'binge', sometimes called a 'Black Mass' by the sailors. The Admiralty then provided the final official rubberstamp for the issue of grog in an order of 1756, though officers were still allowed to take their rum undiluted, hence their ration was called 'neaters'.

According to popular legend Vernon, nicknamed 'Old Grogram' from his habit of wearing a black waterproof coat made of grogram (a mix of silk, mohair and wool, stiffened with gum to waterproof it) provided his sailors with a ready name for the mixture of rum and water: 'grog'. The word became so synonymous with Vernon and his sailors that in 1781 one Thomas Trotter, surgeon on HMS *Berwick*, penned:

A mighty bowl on deck he drew,
And filled it to the brink;
Such drank the Burford's gallant crew,
And such the gods shall drink.

The sacred robe which Vernon wore
Was drenched within the same;
And hence his virtues guard our shore,
And Grog derives its name.

Some sources have tried to predate the word 'grog' to 1718 and Daniel Defoe's book *The Family Instructor, Part II,* in which a former slave boy Toby remarks that in the West Indies the 'black mans ... make the sugar, make the grog, much great work, much weary work all day long.' In fact, as Michael Quinion's investigations (www.worldwidewords.org) discovered, the text is actually 'makee the sugar, makee the ginger'. Another attempt to predate Vernon with the word 'grog' appearing in a popular ballad is similarly rebutted. So until someone comes up with conclusive evidence to the contrary, I am with Old Grogram.

In modern-day cocktail bars grog remains on the menu, though in a slightly different guise. If you mix dark rum, sugar, lime, water (usually carbonated) and a sprig of mint the result is a Mojito cocktail, and a drink not too far away from the sailor's grog. Of course, if you do drink too many you might end up feeling a bit **'groggy'**!

The Black Day

Is this phrase referring to some catastrophic naval defeat or the sinking of a famous ship? No, in fact, the story is far worse. The Black Day of the Royal Navy occurred on 31 July 1970. It was the day the service stopped the issue of rum. In the mid-nineteenth century the size of the daily rum ration or tot had been reduced from a half to a quarter of a pint. The tot was abolished for officers (1881) and warrant officers (1918) until finally the ritual was performed for the last time in 1970, the reason given being that rum does not mix well with complex mechanical equipment and nuclear weapons. It is interesting that more than a century prior to the Black Day, the United States Navy rum ration ceased in 1862. (A variant of the phrase is **'The Black Tot Day'**.)

Bleed/suck the monkey

With the issue of grog playing a big part in keeping sailors reasonably happy with their lot, it is no surprise to find that inventive individuals tried to circumvent the process for distributing spirits. These two phrases reflect those attempts and are often used interchangeably for the process of obtaining spirits surreptitiously. It seems, however, that there are distinct differences in original usage of the terms.

To 'suck the monkey' does not relate to any violation of small furry mammals, nor does it refer to the bundles of cash carried by cockney wideboys; £500 being called a 'monkey'. The monkey in this slang phrase begins deep in the mists of storytelling. Across Medieval Europe there were several versions of bestiary fables; tales of animals acting as, and lampooning, humans. A particularly favourite character was Reynard the Fox. Reynard, befitting his place in the animal kingdom, was a cunning trickster, a player of pranks, who combined a wicked and vicious streak with the ability to charm his way out of sticky situations. In the Germanic versions of stories there is a character called Martin the Ape, and his son is called Moneke, perhaps ultimately derived from the Arabic word for monkey *maimun*, though the name does not appear in any other versions. In the 1481 English translations of the stories by William Caxton, a monkey king falls for a trap set by Reynard.

The monkey was a familiar sight in medieval pageants and fairs. In the abhorrent practice of bear baiting, a monkey would often be seen riding on the back of the bear prior to the event. Moreover, monkey baiting was a popular pastime and fights would be set up, usually with dogs. As a monkey would look quite small when faced with a dog and most certainly while perched on the back of a bear, the word became used colloquially to describe anything that was small, from the short sailor's 'monkey jacket' to the children known as '**powder monkeys**' who were responsible for keeping a ship's guns supplied with powder. 'Monkey' was also used when referring to the small casks that were brought up on deck for the issue of rum. When they were 'bleeding the monkey' sailors would be extracting the rum or other spirits by sneakily boring a small hole into the barrel. The phrase 'sucking the monkey', however, seems to be used more in relation to the practice of acquiring booze ashore, either for immediate consumption or to be smuggled aboard ship. In Captain Marryat's *Peter Simple* the hero finds that while commanding a working party ashore in Barbados, his men take a particular liking to coconut milk purchase from the local inhabitants. Soon after, Simple finds his men 'instead of rolling casks, began to roll themselves in all directions'. Puzzled by this outbreak of apparent illness from drinking coconut milk, which the men explain away as sunstroke, Simple asks Mr Falcon. Falcon replies:

> '*Do you know what "sucking the monkey means"? ... It is a term used among seamen for drinking rum out of cocoa-nuts, the milk having been poured out and the liquor substituted. Now do you comprehend why your men are tipsy?*'

Realising what has gone on, Simple resolves not to allow his men to buy coconuts from the locals again.

In both 'bleeding' and 'sucking' the device for extracting the liquor was called a 'monkey pump', described by Admiral Smyth as, 'Straws or quills for sucking the liquid from a cask, through a gimlet-hole made for the purpose – a practice as old as the time of Xenophon'. Xenophon himself has this to say in *Anabasis*:

> *... wine made from barley in great big bowls; the grains of barley malt lay floating in the beverage up to the lip of the vessel, and reeds lay in them, some longer, some shorter, without joints; when you were thirsty you must take one of these into your mouth, and suck.*

So, whatever it was called in Xenophon's time, the practice of bleeding or sucking the monkey is certainly a time-honoured one!

Down the hatch

This colloquial phrase means the act of drinking, particularly taking a large swig to finish a drink or completely draining a tot. In fact the correct term should be down the hatchway, which is the opening in a deck to allow vertical access. The actual hatch is the covering of a hatchway. The phrase seems to be a recent addition to slang terminology and probably relates to the procedure of loading up the hold of ship by lowering cargo through the hatchways.

Binge

> *'Oh, really? Did it ever occur to you that this recent antique-buying binge you've been on is nothing but a way of sublimating your frustrated sexual desires?'*
>
> Dr Frasier Crane, *Frasier*

Open any newspaper and you will probably find at least one reference to the apparent 'binge drinking' epidemic that has become commonplace in Britain's towns. In 2003 a government health report found that Britain's 'binge drinking' culture was costing the country £20 billion per year. 'Binge drinking' is the practice of drinking as much as possible in the shortest possible with the intention of becoming intoxicated, and often leads to drunken incidents of violence and anti-social behaviour. But it is not a new phenomenon. The casual observer in any port town during the age of sail would have found much the same: a high number of drunken men and women fighting, cavorting and generally up to no good. Although the word can be applied to other activities, e.g. eating, drug taking and furniture buying, it is most commonly associated with drinking. Which is appropriate, as that is where it came from.

In fact, it comes as no surprise to learn that the sailor would sometimes 'binge' himself, for the word means to 'soak'. It seems to have appeared in dialectic use in the mid-nineteenth century, and it appears in Smyth's *Sailor's Word Book*. Once the grog had been drained, the residue left in the cask was called 'plushers' and this was required to be poured into the 'scuppers' and hence overboard. In order to get at any alcohol remaining in this or any other empty spirit cask, the cunning sailor could binge it; soak or rinse it with water in the hope the resulting mix would contain some alcohol. It was also called 'bulling a cask', though as it was usually a rather unsuccessful procedure it was sometimes known as 'Flogging the Monkey'.

Splice the main brace

On occasion it was considered good form to reward the men upon the successful completion of some tricky or dangerous task. One of these tasks gave the world this famous phrase, so beloved of pirate literature and film. In its true form it means to grant the ship's crew a celebratory tot, though in modern-day usage it can refer to an authorised booze-up.

The main brace ran from the main yard to the deck, and was used to position the yard to which was attached the main sail of a square-rigged sailing ship. The main sail was the largest and most important sail; hence the main brace was the largest and heaviest piece of rigging and was constructed of thick, quality cordage. If the main brace failed, a very rare occurrence, the quickest way to repair it was to splice it, i.e. to unravel the ends and then weave in a new piece of rope. The main brace was a long piece of rope which ran through several blocks, and if it was cut required a long piece of rope to be spliced in, so it would have been very hard work. Moreover, the main brace was integral to sailing the ship; if it was carried away the ship would have to keep to the same tack: not a particularly pleasant predicament in bad weather or battle. So, no matter what the weather conditions were like and even if enemy cannon and musket balls were flying through the air, the main brace had to be repaired. And it had to be done quickly and correctly. Only the most experienced and reliable sailors would be detailed for this task and were directly supervised by the boatswain. The rope would be permanently weakened by this procedure, so it is likely the entire main brace would have been replaced at the earliest convenient opportunity.

Once the task had been completed, the men were provided with an extra rum ration by way of a reward thereby giving us the phrase 'Splice the main brace' as the slang for a special spirit issue to the crew. Historically, the term has been used to mark victories, such as at the end of the Second World War, Royal weddings and births or the ascension of a new sovereign. Originally the captain of a ship could order the issuing of the extra tot, but today it remains the preserve of the Monarch and the Board of Admiralty. In June 2005, after the International Fleet Review, the Queen finished her message of thanks with the instruction 'Splice the Mainbrace'.

Nelson's blood

> *Oh, a drop of Nelson's blood wouldn't do us any harm*
>
> 'A drop of Nelson's Blood', sea shanty

As one would expect there are many myths surrounding the issue of rum in the Royal Navy. Ashore, rum is often called 'Nelson's blood'; but why? It was certainly not because Nelson was a particularly big drinker, in fact he usually watered down his glass of wine at dinnertime. The story only appears after Nelson's death at Trafalgar on 21 October 1805. To preserve his body during the voyage home, Nelson's corpse was stripped of all clothing but his shirt, placed in a large cask and covered with spirits. And here the legend starts, for upon arrival back in England it was rumoured that the presence of Nelson's mortal remains had not prevented the ever inventive sailors '**bleeding the monkey**', in effect drinking a heady mix of Nelson's blood and rum.

This tall tale is still popular today, but the facts tell a different story. For starters, eyewitness accounts state Nelson's body was actually preserved in brandy, not rum. Secondly, the cask containing the body had been lashed to the deck of HMS *Victory* and was kept under guard. In addition to this, new brandy was fed into the top while some was drawn off at the bottom. 'On the 24th,' *Victory*'s Surgeon William Beatty informs us, 'there was a disengagement of air from the body to such a degree, that the sentinel became alarmed on seeing the head of the cask raised: he therefore applied to the Officers, who were under the necessity of having the cask spiled to give the air a discharge'. While all this disproves the popular theory as to the origin of the term, there is no concrete evidence as to when or where the phrase 'Nelson's Blood' did originate.

The sun's over the yardarm

The sailor's day involved the consumption of a fair quantity of alcohol, with the entitlement of eight pints of beer spread out across the working day. It would often include beer at breakfast time. As officers did not usually drink beer, they would have to wait for the morning rum tot issued between 10:00 am and midday. In northern waters this just about coincided with the rising summer sun passing the top yardarm (the extreme ends of the yard from which were hung the sails) on a sailing ship. Any officer who did have a drink before this time would incite contempt from his peers, but once the sun had gone over the yardarm it was acceptable for the officers to take an alcoholic drink.

A rather fanciful story entitled 'The sun whose rays ...' from the *Chambers Journal* of 1945, nevertheless illustrates the point precisely:

... since neither of us appears to be lacking in imagination, let us agree that the sun is over the yard-arm!

The Nautical expression was not lost on the 'man-in-the-street.' With the speed of light, his full five senses descended to the immediate vicinity of a certain diluted distillation, the supply of which was getting alarmingly shorter and shorter. 'A little refreshment would not go amiss,' he remarked, not without a sign of enthusiasm.

The precise origin of the phrase remains obscure, and as Covey Crump points out, the correct term is 'fore yard' not 'yard arm'. The phrase certainly seems to pre-date Nelson's time, but one of the earliest references to it in print comes from William Hamilton Maxwell's 1844 *Wanderings in the Highlands and Islands*:

At sea, when the bell is stuck at noon, the sun is said to be 'over the fore-yard'; and then all good men, and true – barring teetotallers – indulge in a glass of grog, if it be their pleasure.

Celebrate the siege of Gibraltar

The sailor does not usually need an excuse to have a drink: nor does many a naval officer. But if either should find themselves in the rather uncomfortable situation of having to come up with a reason, perhaps tea with a dear old aunt, or a visit from the vicar, then none is better than to remember a historic event: for who could argue with that? As the 14 sieges of Gibraltar covered so great a period, from the first siege in 1309 when King Ferdinand IV of Castile captured the place to the last proper military siege in 1779, it is safe to regard any day in the year as an anniversary of a siege of Gibraltar.

On the subject of toasting, no drink in the wardroom (officers' mess) would be complete without an appropriate toast. Here is what officers in Nelson's navy toasted:

Sunday – 'Absent friends'
Monday – 'Our ships at sea'
Tuesday – 'Our men'
Wednesday – 'Ourselves'
Thursday – 'A bloody war or a sickly season', i.e. promotion.
Friday – 'A willing foe and sea room'
Saturday – 'Sweethearts and wives', followed by the response, 'May they never meet'.

And of course, there is the loyal toast to the Monarch, in today's Royal Navy just two words: 'The Queen'.

Three sheets to the wind

Stop thirty years of privilege and tradition. I'd rather have them three sheets to the wind than face a mutiny.

Captain Jack Aubrey, *Master and Commander: The Far Side of the World* (2003)

Although ships' logbooks habitually record incidents with the term 'drunkenness', the sailor himself must have had an assortment of phrases to describe this condition. Certainly one of them has passed ashore and even reached the anodyne world of US television: David Kirsch, fitness guru on *Extreme Makeover* and personal trainer to the stars, admitted to *USA Today* in April 2008 that just one drink and he is 'three sheets to the wind'. More appropriately, beer journalist Pete Brown entitled his 2006 book about a personal quest for the meaning of beer, *Three Sheets to the Wind*.

Of course, most people know that to be three sheets to the wind is to be drunk, in fact, to be very drunk indeed. On board a sailing ship the sheets were the ropes that were attached to the bottom corners of each square-rigged sail. Their purpose was to provide some control over the amount of wind the sail was catching. Correctly attached, the sheets kept the sail taut allowing it to fill with wind and therefore helped to control speed and heading. If the sheets were carried away or allowed to run free, the sail would flap uncontrollably in the wind – a situation called 'having a sheet in the wind'. If several sheets, let's say three, were in this state, the ship might be difficult to control and steer a ragged course like the inebriated sailor, having spent all his 'beer tickets' (local currency), wildly veering from side to side and unable to walk in a straight line (which must have been a sight common in just about every port town across the globe).

Minesweeping

The naval mine has a long history, stretching back to fourteenth-century China. But it was not until the World Wars of the twentieth century that the naval mine made an explosive impact upon naval warfare. A mine is a floating device that detonates when close to or in contact with a ship. They can be left in floating minefields to prevent the passage of enemy ships, or to protect one's own coastline. As they hole a ship below the waterline, they

are a particularly effective weapon. In the first few months of the First World War the *King George V* class battleship HMS *Audacious* was sunk off the coast of Ireland by a German mine. Even today mines still pose a problem for commercial shipping and naval vessels. During the First Gulf War two American ships, USS *Princeton* and USS *Tripoli*, were damaged by Iraqi mines. One of the tasks of a navy is to clear away these mines and to do this specialist ships were built called minesweepers. These ships dragged a wire behind them that would cut the mooring line of the mine, it could then be recovered or disposed of.

It is the sweeping nature of this procedure that has led to the phrase 'minesweeping' coming ashore to describe the, rather disagreeable and potentially dangerous, process of sweeping a pub, club or bar for the leftover parts of other people's drinks.

Sippers, gulpers and sandy bottoms

In the Royal Navy there are a number of ways one can drink an alcoholic beverage. The first is called 'sippers'. This is an age-old practice where one sailor allows another to take a sip from his tot, either as payment for a debt, as a favour or celebration, usually a birthday. With sailors having little or no access to cash, the rum tot was one of the main forms of currency. Although this was an illegal practice, it was recognised by the hierarchy that banning it was virtually unenforceable. So it was 'managed' by allowing the exchange to take place at the rum tub, where officers could keep an eye on things to make sure they did not get out of hand. Where it was not managed it could lead to some serious cases of drunkenness. One submariner recalled that he was:

> … *out for three days, because it's a tradition in the navy you have 'sippers' on your 21st birthday – and it's rum as well! In fact I don't drink, but you had to then because it was the tradition. And every time they gave me a drink of water it tasted like rum. I've never drunk any since. I wasn't in trouble because in a submarine you can get away with it. I was in a bunk at the back in the stokers' mess. It wasn't my fault! My shipmates covered for me saying I was not very well, and they covered my watches.*

One level up is 'gulpers', a substantial single swig by a mate from another's ration. The next stage is a serious undertaking: 'sandy bottoms' which is to drain the whole tot or drink in one go. This was a rare indulgence, and must have been in repayment for a very big favour or debt.

Gin pennant/pendant

In the Royal Navy it is customary for an officer to celebrate good news, perhaps a promotion, birthday or birth of a baby, by entertaining the ship's officers in the wardroom. In order to communicate this very interesting news to officers on the ship, or to invite officers from other ships with the promise of free booze, a ship will fly a special, but unofficial flag. This usually takes the form of a pennant shaped flag consisting of vertical green/white/green sections. In case any officer is unsure of the precise nature of this signal, most pennants will usually display a green cocktail glass on the white background. With the 'gin pendant' now flying it would be rude not to partake of a beverage or two and for that we will need a drinks menu.

Alcoholic Drinks

Piss

This is a very popular term used by Antipodeans to describe beer, or more specifically, lager. Which is quite ironic, as most northern-hemisphere drinkers think of fizzy Australian lagers in the same way. In the Royal Navy one way to dispense such drinks is to fill a soda dispenser with beer or lager and drink from that – this is called an **Iron Lung**.

Starboard light/sticky green

Favoured phrases used by officers to order a crème de menthe.

Hanky panky

Ashore this means a bit of slap and tickle, and presumably it was with this in mind that Madonna sang of her love of hanky panky. In the wardroom, however, it means brandy and ginger wine and, due to the warming nature of the drink, is quite popular in colder climes.

Horse's neck

A little bit different to a hanky panky, this drink combines brandy and ginger ale.

Lion's neck/warrant officers champagne

If rum is mixed with ginger ale instead of brandy it produces this drink.

Gimlette
A tasty mix of gin and lime cordial. Sir Thomas Gimlette joined the Royal Navy in 1879 as a surgeon and convinced his messmates that the best way to take anti-scorbutic lime juice was in this form. What a chap!

Dark and dirty
Pusser's rum mixed with Coke.

Prairie oyster
If too many alcoholic drinks had been consumed the previous evening the sailor could resort to this fine hangover cure. Port wine mixed with an unbroken egg yolk, with mustard, Worcester sauce and some pepper to season: it is suggested that the best way to drink this concoction is 'sandy bottoms'.

Non-alcoholic Drinks

Goffer
Any non-alcoholic fizzy drink, e.g. lemonade.

Corkscrew
An old favourite, water mixed with lime cordial and a dash of Angostura bitters. As the last ingredient was free, this drink appealed to the sailor's mindset of always trying to get something for nothing.

Jubey
Used by Australian and New Zealand sailors it refers to any fruit-flavoured cordial drink.

Bombay oyster
On the other hand if a sailor is suffering from other problems, he could try this laxative. Into a glass of milk, add caster oil, stir, drink and proceed to the nearest head.

Kye
A favourite on cold nights, this is hot chocolate made from chocolate shavings and water or milk to produce a sweet, hot cocoa hit.

8

ACTION STATIONS!

Warships were built to fight. But naval battles do not occur that often; in the French Revolutionary and Napoleonic Wars there were only six major fleet actions during the entire conflict of 1793–1815. The First World War saw only one real fleet-to-fleet encounter, at Jutland in 1916, though there were a number of smaller actions. More frequent are single ship-to-ship actions or small squadron actions, but even these were not that common until the Second World War when combat became a more regular occurrence. In fact, some of the most famous warships in history never fired their big guns in anger: HMS *Warrior*, HMS *Dreadnought* (though she did ram and sink a U-boat), HMVS *Cerberus* and the USS *Arizona* to name just a few.

Yet combat was the ultimate test of a warship and her crew. The warship developed out of the need to provide a specialist fighting platform. In antiquity the Phoenicians, Egyptians and the early Greeks used galleys as both trading vessels and warships until the emergence of the purpose-built war galley mentioned in the Homeric epics. These ships carried sails for general use, but oars were the primary source of propulsion in combat. Ancient sea battles could be large affairs; at Salamis in 480 BC it is estimated that the Greeks mustered over 350 ships, while the invading Persian fleet was twice that number. This form of combat at sea was really an extension of fighting on land; crews would board enemy ships and engage in hand-to-hand combat. So much so that the Romans added the *corvus* to their ships, this was essentially a bridge that could be lowered to allow the troops to pour into an enemy vessel. Additional support was provided by missile troops. The galley continued to be the major naval weapon system in the Mediterranean right up to 1571 when the Battle of Lepanto, fought between Christian forces and Ottoman Empire, became the last naval engagement to be fought purely by oar-powered vessels.

In the meantime, an alternative, sturdier, approach to warship design had occurred in more unpredictable northern waters. During the Dark Ages the Vikings, those famous navigators and exponents of aggressive warfare, combined trading and fighting capabilities into their sea-going longships. Despite retaining a bank of oars, primary propulsion was provided by the more energy-efficient sail. Although not too dissimilar to the Mediterranean war galley, the sail became more important through the development of masts, rigging and spars, eventually producing the full sailing rig. This came out of a need to provide increased space for tradeable goods – oars and oarsmen took up valuable space. Ship types such as the hulk and the cog developed, which in turn led to the carrack, the predecessor of the masted sailing warship. Yet, at the same time as the galley reigned supreme in the Mediterranean and the Northerners started to develop the sailing ship, further East the Chinese had been producing technically superior vessels for centuries culminating in the ocean-going sail-powered 'junk'.

Maritime trade provided a good target for enemy ships so protection was offered by the development of 'forecastles' and 'aftercastles' which could be manned by missile and hand-to-hand-combat troops. This basic layout changed with the introduction, tentatively at first, of cannon. Soon ships began to carry cannon on their sides and it was a logical step to cut holes – gun ports – in the hull thereby giving us the classic sailing man-of-war battleship. Tactics developed slowly, and were evolutionary rather then revolutionary. In 1588 the Spanish Armada still concentrated on close-range boarding tactics, whereas the English ships kept their distance peppering the Spanish fleet (somewhat ineffectually) with shot. Moreover, battles that so far had consisted of a number of single-ship fights gave way to the classic eighteenth-century line-of-battle. In turn that led Nelson, and others, to try to break the line, a tactical process which reached its zenith at the Battle of Trafalgar in 1805.

In the latter half of the nineteenth century the industrial revolution brought about a major change in warship design. Turret-mounted breech-loading guns, steam propulsion and iron protection gave the world a series of bizarre experiments in ship design until in 1906 the Royal Navy's all-big-gun HMS *Dreadnought* rendered every single warship in the world out of date. With the introduction of the submarine and air power in the twentieth century the battleship had met its match, as the greater reach of the carrier reigned supreme in the vast areas of the Pacific during the Second World War. Unrestricted submarine warfare made every vessel on the sea a potential target and led to a host of counter measures and new ship designs. Today, although navies retain their aircraft carriers and strategic nuclear submarines, there is a marked trend towards smaller, more specialised craft, capable of projecting a maritime force ashore into the world's trouble spots.

Finally, one must not forget the human element. For every combat has its casualties; many men who went to sea did not come home again. From the vivid and horrifying 'butcher's shambles', as one eyewitness described the scene on a man-of-war, to those, whether above the waves or below, who simply disappeared into its depths, the sea has demanded a huge toll from the sailor.

Action stations!

This shipboard call to action sends every man to his assigned place ready for battle. It is the highest state of readiness on board Royal Navy vessels. Ashore we use the phrase in a similar way, to prepare or make ready for an event. For example, in June 2006 the Royal Ascot racecourse was reopening after a £200m facelift and so *The Times* previewed the opening with an article entitled, 'Ascot Takes up Action Stations for Grandest of Openings'.

In Nelson's time the process was called 'beat to quarters', the ship's drummers would beat out a pattern of drumbeats. On HMS *Amazon* in 1799 the captain decided, 'The beat of drum for repairing to quarters will be the grenadiers march'. The main deck would be cleared, all unnecessary equipment and kit was stowed away and the guns loaded and primed ready for action. Each man would then take his station. On board ship the men were divided into divisions, each under the command of a lieutenant who was responsible for their health and welfare. To carry out certain tasks, tacking, mooring, getting under way, the men were assigned a specific station: at the cables, or working the sails. All this was listed in the ship's quarter bill, which also included the different stations to be taken up by each member of the crew in battle. The Admiralty required each captain to draw up the quarter bill prior to his ship sailing 'for quartering the officers and men, distributing them to the great guns, small arms, rigging etc.' To ensure there was no confusion he was to draw up a '… general table, expressing the men's names and their respective quarters to be hung up in some public place of the ship, but also particular bills of parchment to be fixed in every quarter and over every gun, containing the men's names appointed to each quarter'.

For many on board a man-of-war this would be beside a gun; for instance in a 36-gun frigate, approximately 74 per cent of the crew would be stationed at the guns. The number of men for each type of gun was usually eight men to each pair of 12-pounders; eleven for each pair of 18-pounders; and fourteen for each pair of the 32-pounders. They were assigned to pairs of guns, one on the starboard and one on the port side, as the ship, carrying its main armament along its sides, was expected to be fighting only on one side at a time. This is the main reason why doubling an enemy ship with two of one's own ships, as happened at the Battle of the Nile in 1798, was a key naval tactic. Quite often

specific men would be called away for certain duties during action; men whose names were marked with a 'B' could be called on deck to repel boarders. Others had 'F', to form part of a fire-fighting party, or 'P', operate the pumps if the ship was taking on water. Of course, the captain and certain officers would direct the ship from the quarterdeck. The system was designed so that each man knew what he was supposed to do in every situation.

When drums were replaced by sirens or bugles in the nineteenth century, the call for the process of preparing the ship for action changed to 'Action Stations!' and is still used by today's Royal Navy. The United States Navy prefers the call 'general quarters' to get the ship ready for action. In the Royal Navy the call 'general quarters' sends every man to his general station and could be for a number of reasons. This caused some confusion for Sub-Lieutenant P. W. Bowyer-Smith onboard HMS *Marlborough* at the Battle of Jutland in 1916 when General Quarters (GQ) was sounded:

> *It was a mistake, and the bugle should have sounded 'Action' not 'GQs', which is an exercise action. Having reported Y Turret cleared away, I looked out and saw that* Iron Duke *was flying the signal to prepare for action in every respect … None of this created any stir at all, as we have done and undone it so often, that it has ceased to be a disappointment when nothing comes of it.*

Robert Lagane of the French Submarine *Iris* summed up the panic that the call to action could produce when the French fleet at Toulon was attacked by the Germans in November 1942:

0405 – The klaxon gave the General Alarm. The watch-keeper on the bridge shouted down the voice pipe: 'Action stations, boys! Fritz is in the Arsenal. Action stations! The bastards have come. They're everywhere! They're shooting everything. Action stations. My God, they're blowing up the base. That one just missed Vénus's arse! Action stations!'

In times of danger, men could be at their action stations for prolonged periods of time, and officers sometimes allowed small groups to stand down for a few minutes to take refreshments. On the morning of the battle of Trafalgar, the British fleet formed up for the attack at 6.40 a.m., but in the light winds could only make about 3 knots. To break up the tedious approach, the men on HMS *Victory* partook of a dinner of pork and wine after they had been 'beat to quarters' at 11.00. The fleet finally entered the action around noon with the *Victory* entering the fray about 20–25 minutes later.

Quarters

The term 'quarters' must be looked at in a bit more depth, as it crops up many times in nautical language. We all know that a quarter is a fourth measure, i.e. a quart of ale is one quarter of a gallon. But many other things at sea are described using the word. Perhaps most pertinent is wind direction. Sailors describe wind direction as blowing from a 'quarter' while 'quarter points' are subdivisions of a compass. A ship is said to be divided into quarters, according to Smyth, 'This term literally implies one quarter of the ship, but in common parlance applies to 45° abaft the beam'. The small boats that sailing ships carried abaft the mizzen mast were called quarter boats. And we also have the quarterdeck, from where the commander of a ship would exercise control.

The term is also commonly used when describing the position of two ships, for instance in Winfield Scott Schley's account of the Battle of Santiago, 3 July 1898, fought between American and Spanish fleets:

At 10.05 – The Brooklyn began to turn with the port helm, and made a complete turn to the eastward, continuing around, so that when again heading west the two leading enemy's ships bore well on her starboard quarter.

The word 'quarter' itself is derived from the French *quartier* and Latin *quartarius*, both referring to the measurement of a fourth part of the whole.

At close quarters

In naval warfare to fight 'at close quarters' is to be right up next to an opponent. This was the way that sea fights were decided from the Classical period until the effective introduction of naval cannon in the sixteenth century. The navies of the Greeks, Romans, Carthaginians, Byzantines, Genoese, Venetians and Spaniards all used galleys, oar-powered vessels designed to ram into an opponent or shear off their oars. The combat would then be decided by close-range missile fire or boarding and hand-to-hand combat.

Fighting at close quarters continued into the age of sail. At the battle of Trafalgar, Nelson's entire plan was designed to get the British fleet into close-quarter action with the enemy where superior discipline and gunnery would be the deciding factor in a 'pell-mell' battle. In his Tactical Memorandum of 1803, he described the idea:

> *The business of an English commander-in-chief being first to bring the Enemy's fleet to battle on the most advantageous terms to himself (I mean that of laying his ships close on board the enemy as expeditiously as possible and secondly to continue them there without separating until the business is decided), I am sensible beyond this object it is not necessary that I should say a word, being fully sensible that the admirals and captains of the fleet I have the honour to command will, knowing my precise object, that of a close and decisive battle...*

And he reinforced this tactic in 1805 with the simple dictum, 'no Captain can do very wrong if he places his Ship alongside that of an Enemy'. Fighting like this was a horrific experience for all involved. Marine Lieutenant Lewis Rotely was on HMS *Victory*'s middle gun deck at Trafalgar:

> *A man should witness a battle in a three-decker from the middle deck, for it beggars all description: it bewilders the senses of sight and hearing. There was the fire from above, the fire from below, besides the fire from the deck I was upon, the guns recoiling with violence, reports louder than thunder, the decks heaving and the sides straining. I fancied myself in the infernal regions, where every man appeared a devil.*

The action between HMS *Shannon* and the USS *Chesapeake* (see below) took place at a distance of around 40 yards. Sometimes the distance was closer; at Trafalgar the crew of HMS *Tonnant* (the same one captured from the French at the Nile in 1798) had to direct their fire-fighting pump onto their opponent, the French ship *Algeciras,* to prevent the muzzle flashes setting fire to both ships. It was not uncommon for ships to become locked together as masts, rigging and yards went over the sides. Close-quarter fighting allowed a crew to board an enemy vessel and seize control. Smyth again: 'Close-quarters may be on any point, and the seaman rather delights in the bow attack, using the bowsprit as his bridge'. Combat at this range was horrendous: 'it is shocking to see many brave seamen mangled so, some with their heads half shot away, others with their entrails mashed lying panting on the deck'.

As gunnery ranges moved from yards to miles in the nineteenth century, close-quarter combat at sea moved to the backburner of mainstream naval doctrine until the introduction of torpedoes, torpedo boats and submarines. Once again, ranges closed down to yards, and in some cases actual touching distance, the brave Chariot crews of the Second World War would submerge and sail under a warship to attach limpet mines to the hull of enemy vessels.

'Close quarters' were actually specific parts of a ship where hand-to-hand fighting was expected to take place. This area, between the foremast and mainmast was reinforced with barriers of wood and loop-holed to allow musket fire. As the fighting took place in these quarters, they gave their name to this mode of combat. Ashore close-quarter fighting is still taught to the world's combat forces. Metaphorically, we usually use the term to describe something that happens very close to us. For instance *The Scotsman* remarked of the new £5.6m chimp house at Edinburgh Zoo, 'The joy of this building is that it makes it so easy for visitors to watch the animals at close quarters'. The second modern usage is to describe a confined space, derived from the use of the word 'quarters' in relation to a dwelling space.

Nail one's colours to the mast

> *Miss Matty and Miss Pole had been visitors on this occasion for many years; and now they gallantly determined to nail their colours to the mast, and to go through Darkness Lane rather than fail in loyalty to their friend.*
> *Cranford* by Elizabeth Gaskell

Today when we see this phrase we think of the process of making a public show of stubborn resistance, to fight to the last. It could be used by a politician trying to save their career after being caught in some scandal, or perhaps a boardroom heavyweight clinging to their position in the face of poor financial results.

We have already seen a common *ruse de guerre* in naval warfare was to '**sail under false colours**'. In battle when a captain found his ship in an untenable position and surrender was the only way to prevent further bloodshed, he would signal his intention by lowering (called striking) his colours. Upon seeing this, enemy vessels would (hopefully) cease firing and undertake measures to take control of the ship. But the nature of naval battle made it a rather unpredictable and gruesome environment. Amongst the carnage of broken bodies, blood-washed decks, limbs and entrails, the colours of a ship could often be shot away. This could dishearten the men and give the enemy hope that defence was slackening. In this situation there was only one course of action: to nail the colours to a mast to indicate the fight would go on. On the other hand, the act could be used as a statement of intent, as Frederick Marryat pointed out in *Poor Jack*:

> *The Captain now came forward as red as a turkey-cock; he said nothing –*
> *looked at the vessel – and then turned as white as a sheet.*
> *'She's more than our match, if she's an enemy,' said he.*
> *'I should rather think not, sir,' replied Bramble. 'All you have to do is make*
> *your men fight, and nail your colours to the mast.'*

While this example comes from naval literature, there are real instances of ships nailing their colours to the mizzen mast. Louis Lebreton's dramatic image of the French 80-gun ship *Tonnant* at the battle of the Nile, 1 August 1798, shows the vessel dismasted and with her colours flying from the mizzen mast. This reflected the fighting spirit of her commander, Aristide Aubert Du Petit Thouars, who, despite losing both legs and an arm, remained on deck commanding his ship lodged upright in a barrel of wheat. His dying commands were for his crew not to surrender the ship. Two years later, in combat with the 80-gun French *Guillaume Tell* on Sunday, 30 March 1800, HMS *Foudroyant*'s log notes, '½ pt. 6 shot away the Enemy's Main & Mizen mast. Saw a Man nail the Colours to the stump of the Mizen Mast'.

This is one phrase that really does translate literally into wider usage. All men of war did, and still do, carry national colours, 'ensigns' to give them their correct name, to aid identification. In the Royal Navy this is the famous white ensign, a red cross of St George on a white field and the Union Flag in the upper canton. For the United States Navy it is the Stars and Stripes. The French Navy flies the Tricolore and the Russian Navy a blue saltire on a white field, while the Imperial Japanese Navy flew the infamous red rising sun with 16 rays on a white field.

A *shot across the bows*

The word 'shot' seems to derive from one of any number of Anglo-Saxon and Germanic words and means the projecting of a missile. The bows of a ship are the foremost portion. Therefore, to aim a shot across, or, more commonly, to pass just in front of the bows of a ship was a very obvious warning. We now use this phrase in exactly the same way; a 'shot across the bows' is an intentional and very obvious warning. For example, in this extract from a *Reuters* article of 22 May 2007: '[Chinese Vice Premier] Wu said politicizing differences over trade issues would only make matters worse – a shot across the bows of U.S. lawmakers who threaten to restrict Chinese imports'.

Before the days of effective signalling at sea, Morse code and radio, the only way for one ship to demand another ship to stop was for a shot to be sent across the bows of the latter. Ships would want to stop another ship for several reasons, merchantmen might be stopped to see if they were carrying contraband goods, or a foreign ship in territorial waters might be quizzed. If the ship failed to make any attempt to respond to the shot, by either signalling or heaving to, then she could expect another shot, this time aimed directly at her hull.

Commander Raphael Semmes was in command of the commerce raider CSS *Sumter* during the early months of the American Civil War. In July 1861, sighting a sail in the distance and on course to cross his path, Semmes appeared to ignore the other vessel. Waiting until he had closed to within one mile, he ordered English colours hoisted and the other ship answered with the 'Stars and Stripes' of the United States. Quickly, Semmes hauled down the St George and hoisted the Confederate 'Stars and Bars'. Then 'a shot was

fired across the bows of the astonished Yankee, who at once hove-to, and a boat was sent on board to take possession of the *Sumter*'s first capture'. She was the *Golden Rocket* worth around $30–40,000 bound for Cuba, but with no cargo Semmes took off her crew then burned the Yankee vessel.

It is one of the main reasons why the ships of many modern navies continue to carry close-range weapons. In an increasingly unstable world, the policing of international waters to stamp out piracy, people-smuggling and other illegal practices, to fire a shot across the bows is still an important naval tactic. Sea-launched Tomahawk Missiles or 4.5 calibre heavy weapons are no good to fire across bows of a suspect vessel; a single carefully aimed small calibre shot is required to prevent possible wider political ramifications.

Deliver a broadside

We use this phrase today when a person gives someone a forceful telling off, or puts forward an alternative point of view to an argument.

And while that might be an uncomfortable experience for those on the receiving end, one thing you really did not want to be on the receiving end at sea was a full broadside from a man-of-war, for a 'broadside' is a ship discharging all the guns on one side at the same time. At the battle of Trafalgar HMS *Victory* carried 104 guns:

Lower gun deck:	30 x 32-pounders
Middle gun deck:	28 x 24-pounders
Upper gun deck:	30 x 12-pounders
Quarterdeck:	12 x 12-pounders
Forecastle:	2 x 12-pounders
	2 x 68-pounder carronades

Giving a total broadside weight of shot of 1148lb, which is a lot of metal flying through the air. Moreover, one of her 32lb cannonballs would leave the gun barrel at 1,600 feet per second and penetrate up to 42 inches of solid oak at a range of 400 yards. When *Victory* engaged and raked the French flagship *Bucentaure* at Trafalgar her port 68-pounder carronade unleashed a hail of 500 musket balls and a single round shot through the stern windows of the French flag ship. This was followed by a devastating broadside which destroyed *Bucentaure*'s stern, caused horrific casualties amongst the crew and, in one go, virtually removed the ship from the fight.

The largest broadside ever deployed on a warship belongs to the two behemoths of the Imperial Japanese Navy's *Yamato* Class. They carried 9 x 18.1in .45-calibre monsters, capable of delivering a broadside of 28,971lb. But these giants were outdated before they were even launched; the rise of the aircraft carrier had put paid to the battleship and the broadside, the core of naval tactics for over two centuries, was no more. There was to be one last hurrah for the classic naval broadside; during the First Gulf War the US Navy's *Missouri* and *Wisconsin* fired their 16-inch guns at Iraqi targets on land. Today the broadside is dead; there is not a single battleship in any of the world's navies.

There is another form of broadside that could possibly give us our current usage, the 'broadside ballad'. These were single-sided printed sheets containing the lyrics to popular folk songs, news and general tittle-tattle often sung to music. Broadside ballads date back to the sixteenth century and judging by some of the titles and subject matter, one would not want to hear one of these delivered either: 'A most excellent song of the love of young Palmus and Sheldra'; 'The Wanton Wife of Cattle-Gate' or 'The Boatman's Delight'; 'The Countryman's Lamentation for the Death of his cow'.

Don't give up the ship

This phrase might not be too familiar to a British or European reader, but it is rather popular in North America where it originated. In 1812 deteriorating relations between the United States and Britain led to war. The conduct of the war at sea was controversial to say the least, with the Americans gaining some notable early successes due to their heavier armament. Some redress was made off Boston on 1 June 1813 when HMS *Shannon*, under the command of Captain Philip Broke, encountered the USS *Chesapeake*, Captain James Lawrence. Within a few minutes Broke had dismasted the *Chesapeake*. Lawrence was hit by small-arms fire and mortally wounded. He was carried below allegedly exhorting his crew, 'Don't give up the ship. Fight her till she sinks'. But it was all in vain; *Chesapeake* had been given a sound thrashing and surrendered to a British boarding party. Lawrence was taken captive, but it was clear he was dying and he passed away three days later. The meaning behind Lawrence's words is clear: not to surrender, to keep fighting on against the odds.

Lawrence's dying words were picked up by other American patriots. Three months later on Lake Erie Commodore Oliver Hazard Perry faced a British fleet. With his flagship, the *Lawrence* knocked out; he transferred his battle flag to the *Niagara* and proceeded to win a famous victory. Perry had been a friend of Lawrence and the battle flag in question carried the words 'Don't give up the ship'. The words subsequently moved others to pick up a quill:

> *A hero on his vessel's deck*
> *Lay welt'ring in his gore*
> *And tattered sail, and shattered wreck,*
> *Told that the fight was o'er:*
> *But e'en when death had glazed his eye,*
> *His feeble, quivering lip*
> *Still uttered with life's latest sigh,*
> *'Don't, don't give up the ship.'*
>
> Robert Milledge Charlton, 1839

In 1953 the great cartoon director Chuck Jones put his own unique spin on Lawrence's immortal words. Voiced by Mel Blanc the animated short sees Sam Sheepdog trying to prevent Ralph Wolf from getting his teeth into a flock of sheep. So what else could it be called but *Don't Give up the Sheep*! And Sam delivers in style, finishing the cartoon by spanking Ralph with a wooden club. Readers with a similar interest in naval history and Chuck Jones cartoons might also like to check out the 1954 sequel *Sheep Ahoy* in which Ralph Wolf uses a pedal-powered submarine in an attempt to sneak up on an unsuspecting sheep. Needless to say the scheme is thwarted by Sam Sheepdog, sending Ralph tumbling over a waterfall.

At loggerheads

When people say they are 'at loggerheads' with someone, it means they are in the middle of a dispute, an argument, a fight perhaps, or have reached an impasse. For example, in April 2008 *Der Spiegel* reported, 'Germany and France at Loggerheads over Arms Deal with Libya'.

The phrase comes from a useful tool known as a logger, which was used when caulking the seams of a ship. The pitch used in caulking had to be pliable and this was achieved by heating. One way of doing this was to use the logger, an iron bar with an iron sphere at one end (on occasion there might have been one at each end) and a hook at the other end. The sphere would be heated up then sunk into a bucket of pitch, perhaps the '**hot headed**' aspect of this act was transferred to anyone arguing on board ship. If the ship was boarded by the enemy then it made a handy weapon, akin to a mace, and could deliver a fearful blow. Anyone wielding such an improvised weapon would therefore have been 'at loggerheads' with their foe. Smyth also described this tool as a 'logger-heat', perhaps implying the heating part of the operation might have led to the name. He also gives another, rather different, use on board ship: 'It was also used to pound cocoa before chocolate was supplied'.

The use of bar-shot in naval warfare provides another use of the word logger. The bar-shot was a fiendish device, consisting of two spheres (or sometimes half spheres) joined together by a short bar. When fired into an enemy vessel it would slice through rigging, yards and punch holes through sails; and woe betide any sailor who found himself in the way as it could take off limbs, heads or cut a person clean in two. Some sources suggest it was also called a 'loggerhead' after the caulking tool described above.

Named after the logger, a loggerhead has also been synonymous with anything with a large head. This example sees everyone's favourite Bard using the word to indicate stupidity, in precise terms a blockhead. In Shakespeare's *Taming of the Shrew* Pertuchio asks where his serving men are, they respond with 'here sir' to which Pertuchio laconically remarks:

> *Here, sir! here, sir! here, sir! here, sir!*
> *You logger-headed and unpolish'd grooms!*
> *What, no attendance? no regard? no duty?*
> *Where is the foolish knave I sent before?*

Carrying on with the theme of large heads, 'loggerhead' is also the name of a species of marine turtle present along the American coast, and is also the name of a small bird.

A loose cannon

During the age of sail the primary armament of the warship was the smoothbore cannon. This was attached to a four-wheeled carriage, in turn mounted on a 'truck'. The act of propelling a projectile toward the enemy also generated a fair amount of recoil force. Experiments have shown the recoil distance of one of HMS *Victory*'s 32-pounder guns would be in the region of 50 feet. Obviously, this was not a good thing when her maximum beam (extreme breadth) was only 51 feet! Anyone caught in the way of the gun was in danger of serious injury or death; the barrel of a 32-pounder weighed 6,000lb alone. In order to manage the recoil a system of blocks and

MM

tackle attached the gun to the sides of the ship. This system brought the recoil down to about 11 feet and allowed the gun to be run back out ready for firing again. Moreover, the tackle ensured that the gun could be safely secured in bad weather.

But on occasion guns did break free. Out of control they were entirely unpredictable as they careened round the deck, smashing wood and bone indiscriminately. Compounding the material damage, having such a weight moving around would also affect the stability of the ship. HMS *Defence* was just off the west coast of Jutland on Christmas Eve 1811 when she was caught in the worst storm to hit the area for many years. Inevitably she ran onto offshore reefs. Only six men survived, and one of them, Joseph Page, left a terrifying account. As the ship ran aground the masts went over the side, then: 'The sea breaking her, the dismal shrieks of the people, the guns breaking adrift, and crushing the men to death, rendered the whole a dreadful scene'.

Although taken from fiction, the full horror of a loose cannon is portrayed with considerable force in Victor Hugo's 1874 novel *Ninety-Three*:

> *This is perhaps the most frightful of all accidents at sea. Nothing more terrible can happen to a warship on the open sea and under full sail. A cannon that breaks its moorings suddenly becomes a kind of supernatural beast. It is a machine which transforms itself into a monster. That mass speeds on its wheels, tilts when the ship rolls, plunges when it pitches, goes, comes, stops, seems to meditate, resumes its swift movement, goes from one end of the ship to the other with the speed of an arrow, spins around, slips to*

one side, dashes away, rears up, spins around, slips to one side, dashes away, rears up, collides, smashes, kills, exterminates. It is a battering-ram which attacks a wall according to its own whim.

The unpredictable, dangerous nature of a loose cannon has led to the widespread use of the phrase ashore to describe someone who is outspoken in their views and will not adhere to a corporate identity. It is a phrase often used by political hacks to describe those who will not toe the party line, for example:

> *Is Boris Johnson a loose cannon or a Tory hero?*
> *Telegraph*, 5 October 2006
> *Dole Campaigns for Man He Called 'Loose Cannon'*
> *The New York Times*, 13 September 1994

As these quotes show, although the cannon went out of naval use in the nineteenth century, 'loose cannons' still remain ashore.

9

POKING CHARLIE

To 'Poke Charlie' is to make fun, deride or just simply insult someone or something. Like many naval slang terms the origins are obscured by the passage of time. All we know is that it certainly was, and on occasion still is, used in the Royal Navy. Admiral Sir Bernard Rawlings, commanding the Royal Navy's operations in the Pacific at the end of the Second World War wrote to Admiral Andrew Cunningham in April 1945:

> *Just had a nice signal from [Admiral Chester] Nimitz – what pleased me about it is that so far there is nothing that they can poke Charlie at the White Ensign over. I do mind very much that we came through high in their opinion – it's so absolutely important for our future – indeed I feel it's the most serious side of my job far and away.*

This chapter is a little different from those preceding it. Due to the nature of the subjects covered, it is divided into three parts. The first section considers slang words relating to women, as they are, in the main, derogatory, while the second examines a wider range of insults. The final section lists some of the ruder words and phrases. I hope they will provide a flavour of the colourful language of the lower deck. Some are not for the faint hearted or easily offended – you have been warned!

Women

Despite the popular belief that the navy was no place for a woman, it was not unusual to find women afloat. When a ship was in port the seaman thought he was entitled to one of two things: either to be allowed a run ashore or to have entertainment come to him. In fact, the sailor of Nelson's time had no right to shore leave in home waters because it was an ideal opportunity for men to abscond. Some hands would spend years on board ship without setting foot ashore. In order to manage the inevitable frustration, even anger, this could cause (one of the demands of the men who mutinied at the Nore in 1797 was that they might be allowed ashore), a certain amount of leeway was granted by allowing visitors on to the ship when it was in port. With wives, sweethearts and prostitutes accommodated on board, the lower decks could become quite a scene according to one contemporary source:

> *The whole of the shocking, disgraceful transactions of the lower deck it is impossible to describe – the dirt, filth, and stench; the disgusting conversation; the indecent beastly conduct and horrible scenes; the blasphemy and swearing; the riots, quarrels and fighting.*

Some women even went to sea, sometimes as wives, usually of warrant officers. During action they would act as nurses assisting the surgeon going about his grisly business in the cockpit. On 10 May 1813 Mary Allen and Mary Marshall, wives of seamen, were entered onto the books of Commodore Stephen Decatur's USS *United States*. It seems Decatur had specifically asked for them to serve on board as nurses. In 1803 Commodore Richard Morris of the USS *Chesapeake*, which was headed for the Mediterranean as part of the United States fleet to blockade Tripoli, had obtained permission to take his wife along. One of the sailors, Henry Wadsworth, dryly noted that, 'her person is not beautiful, or even handsome, but she looks very well in a veil'. It was not a success; the Commodore faced an inquiry on his return to America as to why he had spent too much time in port allowing Mrs Morris to socialise, rather than on active operations. Other women could be on board ships as passengers; officers' wives and families heading to destinations overseas such as the West or East Indies would often travel on Royal Navy ships.

Then there are the women that went to sea dressed as men. After the French ship *Achille* blew up at Trafalgar the crew of HMS *Pickle* were rather startled to pull a naked French woman from the water. Jeanette, as she was called, had gone to sea disguised as a man to follow her husband. She saw him killed in action and when *Achille* caught fire had thrown off her clothes before plunging into the water. Brought on board HMS *Victory*, she was dressed in theatre clothing used for entertaining the crew.

The fishing fleet

For many families, marrying off a daughter to a successful navy officer could be a good bit of business. Naval officers on the up might make it to captain and then, hopefully, the promotion system would take its course as the individual moved up through the ranks of admirals. Being married to a successful officer carried a great deal of prestige. Like most things in life money was at the heart of all this. Naval officers' pay could provide a steady income; in Nelson's time a navy captain of a first-rate man-of-war was paid £32.4.0 per month. In 1953 a recently promoted captain would be paid £4.0.0 per day.

In addition there was always the lure of prize money. This was money divided between a ship's crew in reward for capturing an enemy ship. The process dated back to the sixteenth century and was formalised in 1708. The total prize money was divided into eighths then handed out as follows (the system became more complex in 1808):

Two eighths divided between all the hands
One eighth divided between the junior and petty officers and equivalents
One eighth divided between the warrant officers and equivalents
One eighth divided between the lieutenants and equivalents
One eighth to the admiral in command of the squadron – if the orders came from the Admiralty this went to the captain
Two eighths to the captain

The system could produce huge rewards for successful captains. Captain Peter Rainier in the frigate HMS *Caroline* captured the Spanish ship *San Rafael* in 1807. The *San Rafael* carried a very lucrative cargo including $500,000 in specie. Rainier's share of this haul was a whopping £52,000. To put that into context the cost of building a frigate around that time was just around £20,000. In today's money Rainier's £52,000 would be just shy of £1.7 million. The system was changed in 1918 so that all money went into a central pool to be paid out to all naval personnel.

With all this in mind, the collective name for a bevy of available young ladies looking for a suitable and well-off chap is 'the fishing fleet', because they are fishing for husbands. In particular, the term was applied to the patrons of the Ladies Lounge of the Union Club, in Valetta, Malta, the headquarters of the British Mediterranean Fleet until the Second World War.

As well as the patrons, the Union Club had its own nickname due to the presence of the 'fishing fleet': it was called 'The Snake Pit' in homage to the venomous atmosphere generated by so many young ladies competing for attention from young naval officers. It is now used ashore to describe any haunt favoured by naval officers, as it will inevitably attract a fishing fleet.

Poodle faking

This is the time-honoured art of a faking interest in a lady in order to improve one's financial, social or professional position. Junior officers would cultivate the society of females married to their superiors; for instance chatting to and flattering the admiral's wife during a tea party. The officer would be playing the role of a 'lapdog', and ladies of high society with some influence over their husbands, would often choose the poodle as their companion of choice. Hence, when going ashore to indulge in such activities junior naval officers would declare that they were off for an afternoon of 'poodle faking'. The phrase was used by Tristan Jones in *Dutch Treat: A Novel of World War II*: 'She must have been out with that damned poodle-faker Ffoulkes again'. In the early years of the twentieth century 'poodle' was also a slang term for a woman.

Titless wave

In the United States Navy this term relates to a male fulfilling the petty officer rank of yeoman, a position which entails secretarial and clerical duties. During the First World War many women were recruited into this role and by December 1918 there were around 11,000 women serving in the United States Navy. When volunteer women entered the USN during the Second World War they were referred to as 'Women Accepted for Volunteer Emergency Service', which was abbreviated down to WAVES. Hence the rank of yeoman came to be associated with women and so any man ranked as such is a 'titless wave'.

Wrens

Many people will have heard of the WRENS, the Women's Royal Naval Service. During the First World War, in similar fashion to the United States Navy, the Royal Navy recruited women into certain roles, mainly as clerical support, telegraphers and other non-combat roles. The organisation was revived during the Second World War expanding to 75,000 personnel at its peak. WRENS became extinct when the service was absorbed into the Royal Navy in 1993. Today female sailors are still referred to by some as Wrens.

Show a leg

'Show a leg, show a leg,' they shouted to the others and soon had the whole camp astir. 'Remember,' they shouted, 'battle at three o'clock sharp.'

Swallows and Amazons by Arthur Ransome

Despite the presence of so many women on board a ship, when it was moored in port the sailors still had a full day's work to put in. With little spare room on a man-of-war, the wives and sweethearts would have spent the night cuddled up with their sailor in his hammock. As the boatswain's mates went round the gun decks they needed to know which hammocks contained seamen trying to avoid turning out and which still contained women having a lie in. The Boatswain's mate, as a man of the world, would be able to tell the difference between a sailor's leg and the more shapely form of a female leg. Hence he would cry, 'Show a leg or a purser's stocking'. Those legs that were female were left to sleep; those that were not were turned out.

We use the phrase ashore in a similar fashion, for 'to show a leg' means to wake up, get a move on, or make a start. It has become closely associated with, and may indeed be the origin of, the phrase '**shake a leg**', which has a similar meaning.

Insults

Insults are more than just crude or euphemistic swear words. Insults are used to cast aspersions about competence, sexual prowess or parentage. Many of them we still use today. Quite often they relate to minority groups afloat: ethnic minorities, homosexuals and women. Sometimes they refer to less than competent crewmates. This section by no means provides a comprehensive lexicon of all naval insults. The origin of some of the more rude insults is difficult to define. Some undoubtedly started ashore, but as they particularly appeal to seamen I have included some of them here.

Ashore the expression 'swear like a sailor' is used to describe someone who litters his or her everyday conversation with expletives. Despite the reputation the sailor has for coarse language, not all captains tolerated it. In fact, swearing was an offence under the Articles of War. Certain captains picked out specific words, for instance Prince William Henry, Duke of Clarence and the future King William IV, as Captain of HMS *Pegasus* in 1786–88 decreed:

> *As it is but too frequent practice on board His Majesty's ships to make use of that horrid expression bugger, so disgraceful to a British seaman; if any person shall be heard using this expression they may be assured they will be severely punished.*

Perhaps just as relevant and humorous is the sub-genre of insults that are best described as 'Haddockisms' in homage to their most famous proponent: Captain Haddock from the *The Adventures of Tintin* series of comics. When introducing this character to the series the creator Georges Prosper Remi, better known by his *nom de plume* Hergé, wanted to include some of the more colourful language used by sailors. Unable to use real expletives in a children's comic, he hit upon the idea of using words that conveyed the meaning of an insult but were acceptable to the audience (and their parents!). Here are a few choice examples:

> *Ten thousand thundering typhoons!*
> *Miserable blundering barbecued blister!*
> *Lubberscum!*
> *Billions of billious barbecued blue blistering barnacles!*

Landlubber

We all know what a 'landlubber' is: someone who has little or no seafaring experience. The word, however, is not derived from someone who loves the land, as opposed to the sea, as some people think. On a ship some men were there purely for their collective brute strength and were designated as landsmen. The able seamen would naturally look down upon the landsmen, considering them unskilled oafs. This was the original use of the word 'lubber', which dates back to at least the fourteenth century where it was used to describe someone who was clumsy or stupid and may be related to the old Welsh word *llob*, or old German *lob*. 'Lubber' regularly appears in nautical fiction, such as this example from Robert Louis Stevenson's *Treasure Island*:

'Two guineas!' roared Merry, shaking it at Silver. 'That's your seven hundred thousand pounds, is it? You're the man for bargains, aint you? You're him that never bungled nothing, you wooden-headed lubber!'

So, the landlubber was to be unskilled in seamanship as the landsmen were, and it is this meaning that US Congressman Samuel Finley Vinton was alluding to while discussing the Navy Appropriation Bill in 1837:

… living as he did in the State of Ohio, and far in the interior, and knowing nothing of sea service, he was one of these to whom the gentleman's appellative of landlubber would apply; and it was for that reason, which the gentleman had furnished to his hand, that he would not vote for the plan …

Idle

'Well, yes, you see, only the other day, Prime Minister Pitt called me an idle scrounger, and it wasn't until later that I thought how clever it would've been to have said, "Oh, bugger off, you old fart!"'
Prince George, *Blackadder the Third*

To be idle or an idler is to be exceptionally lazy, i.e. to do no work; or not put to use, as in the expression 'bone idle'. Dr Samuel Johnson used this meaning of the word for a series of 104 weekly essays, published between 1758 and 1760, entitled *The Idler*. Society tends to display a deep-rooted suspicion of those who display idle tendencies, as evidenced by the phrase 'the devil makes work for idle hands to do'. In fact the modern word 'idle' seems to come from the old Anglo-Saxon *idel* meaning vain or useless.

Chapter 4 examined the way a ship's crew was divided up. One major distinction was between those experienced hands who were expected to stand watch at night and, as Smyth states, 'all those on board a ship-of-war, who, from being liable to constant day duty, are not subjected to keep the night watch, but must go on deck if all hands are called during the night'. These latter men were classified as 'daymen' and were known by the informal term '**idlers**'. They included non-seamen such as the cook, chaplain, surgeon and carpenter and all their respective crews, servants and mates. Petty officers, such as the boatswain and sail-maker and their mates, were also classified as 'idlers'. Sometimes such men were experienced seamen who were too old to work the tops and had acquired new skills, thereby prolonging their career in the navy.

Sailors recognised that they worked as hard as the rest of the crew, but the fact that idlers could regularly spend an uninterrupted night, tucked up and dozing away in their cots and hammocks perhaps led to the word starting to take on negative connotations. Another explanation is hinted at in Captain Edward Riou's orders for HMS *Amazon* from 1799:

> *Idlers and boys generally require particular attention in order to keep them clean and it is the duty of every man in the ship, as far as it lays in his power, to take notice that dirty boys are not permitted to remain so, but that for the general good he expresses it to his superiors and do his utmost to induce the boys to keep themselves clean and hang up their hammocks and not lie about the decks, by which they become filthy, sickly and useless.*

Nearly every sea officer was allowed servants – these were boys who were sent to sea to learn a trade or, for young gentlemen, obtain some valuable seafaring experience as a way to get to the quarterdeck. As a fair number of them would be classified as idlers the connection between the use of the word 'idle' and the problems experienced by Edward Riou is obvious.

Waister

While we might use the modern word 'waster' in a similar way to 'idle', they are in fact very different. While an idler might be lazy, a 'waister', or 'waster' is someone who intentionally squanders his or her life away. In nautical terms they also have quite different meanings. On board ship, with the best hands working aloft, the least skilled and least intelligent of the crew were the landsmen, who were collected together on deck. Although the more skilled sailors did not have much respect for them, the landsmen provided the brute force necessary for hoisting and hauling. An anonymous publication of 1804 (in fact written by a serving officer called John Davie) noted:

> *The afterguard and waisters are generally composed of indifferent seamen and landmen … These men have not only the burden, but every dirty and inferior duty to execute; to them I conceive an officer's principal attention should be directed.*

This latter statement bears out the reason why such men were collected under the watchful eye of the officers. The easiest place for this was between the forecastle and the quarterdeck, the area known as the 'waist' of the ship, hence the men stationed there became known as 'waisters'.

Snotty

This word is used today to refer to someone who is offensive or insolent or interferes in other people's business. Popular uses include 'snotty nosed' or 'snotty faced'. This is not to be confused with 'snooty' meaning 'arrogant' or 'snobbish', which has its roots in the demeanour of such people holding their noses up (think of a pig's snout).

In April 2008 Russian President Vladimir Putin responded to criticism that he might be about to marry a 24-year-old gymnast with the following diatribe:

> *In what you said, there is not a single word of truth. Nobody should ever interfere in others' private lives. I have always reacted negatively to those who, with their snotty noses and erotic fantasies, prowl into others' lives.*

At sea a 'snotty' (originally 'snottie') was sailor's slang for a midshipman, the lowest-ranking officer on board ship. These boys sometimes went to sea at a very young age and did, literally, grow up at sea, displaying all the attitude of youth: arrogance, tempers, tears and tantrums. Legend has it that one of the less amenable habits of such young boys was to wipe their noses on their sleeves, thereby gaining the nickname 'snottie'. In order to stamp this out three buttons were attached to each cuff.

Life as a midshipman could be a very uncomfortable experience, and with so many young men grouped together acting in high spirits there were any number of cruel, even violent, pranks and games. A midshipman's mess might have its own code of conduct and rituals with violent punishments for those who broke it; bullying of unpopular midshipmen was common. Reminiscing about his own days as a midshipman before the First World War, Captain Charles Walker recalled, 'no one who has been through the mill ever forgets it. When I met a retired Admiral at a reunion dinner, his first remark to me was, "Charles, how I hated those senior snotties in the RESO [HMS *Resolution*]".'

Pipe down

> *'Pipe down, pipe down. This is an operating room. As I was saying, here's to Major Winchester for showing that a man can be neat, clean, and bathed, and still end up smelling bad.'*
>
> Colonel Sherman Potter, *M*A*S*H*

If someone tells you to 'pipe down' they are telling you to shut up, to be quiet. This has some relation to the origin of the phrase. On board a sailing

warship the hammocks, used by sailors to sleep in, would be 'piped up' in the morning. This required the hands to un-sling their hammocks from the clews and take them up on deck to be aired during the day. At the end of the working day the boatswain would signal 'pipe down' as an instruction to the hands to take their hammocks out of stowage and hang them up ready for sleeping. These were strict orders; on board HMS *Indefatigable* in 1812, 'Any hammock found on deck two minutes after they are piped down, the person to whom it belongs is to be reported'. Once the men had been piped down they were expected to go to sleep until roused for their watch. All lights were extinguished and there was to be no smoking; hence the piping down was, quite literally, an order to keep quiet.

There is, however, another slightly different interpretation. If there had been a fracas on deck or some other problem, or the men had been called together, to witness punishment for instance, the men would be sent back to their work by being piped down. For example in Frederick Marryat's *Frank Mildmay or The Naval Officer* the hands were assembled to watch a flogging: 'As soon as the prisoner was cast loose, he commanded to pipe down, or in other words, to dismiss the people to their usual occupations'. This is also the opinion of Smyth who defines 'pipe down' as, 'The order to dismiss the men from the deck when a duty has been performed on board ship'.

Son of a gun

This phrase is used ashore as a mildly rude expression of contempt or surprise, sometimes euphemistically, in polite company or the workplace, to replace something a bit coarser. It can also be used to describe someone committing an act of roguish behaviour.

As it was not uncommon for women to be on board a man-of-war there were obviously occasions when pregnant women gave birth in port or at sea. The only place where this could take place was in the area between two guns, the same area used by the hands for their messes. When the child born afloat was a boy 'one admiral', remarked Smyth, 'declared he literally was thus cradled, under the breast of a gun-carriage' and hence was a true 'son of a gun'. According to Covey Crump such a child was:

> *Begotten in the galley and born under a gun*
> *Every hair a rope yarn, every tooth a marline spike*
> *Every finger a fishhook and his blood right good Stockholm tar*

Births at sea certainly took place. In 1810 the Edinburgh *Annual Review* reported the remarkable story of Sally Trunnion, so called after her place of birth (trunnions were the two-gun barrel supports that rested on the carriage) and therefore presumably a 'daughter of a gun'. The day after her father had been killed in action Sally's mother had died giving birth to her, whereupon the sailors looked after the infant before depositing her at Greenwich Royal Naval Asylum along with £50 raised by the crew. Such events were not confined to the Royal Navy; on the USS *Chesapeake* in 1803 the wife of James Low, captain of the forecastle, gave birth to a baby boy in the boatswain's store.

While such events might point to a valid explanation for the term 'son of a gun', it does not explain why it is used ashore as an insult. In fact, used contemptuously the phrase is designed to cast doubt on the parentage of the individual concerned. This usage of the phrase points to the spaces between the guns on the gun deck being the place of conception rather than the place of birth! With a plethora of loose women entertaining the sailors in port, whether in home waters or abroad, and the likelihood that women who did go to sea indulged in sexual intercourse with sailors, it was inevitable that some would become pregnant. Due to the nature of their work and the number of potential suitors, in some cases it might be impossible to know who the father was. Moreover, some sailors' wives resorted to prostitution as a necessary evil to feed their families and in port towns the most numerous clients would have been sailors from other ships. In these circumstances it is impossible to calculate the number of illegitimate children – all that was known is that the boys certainly were a 'son of a gun'.

Nicknames

Sailors in the Royal Navy have a long tradition of assigning nicknames to each other based on their surnames. Most are from word associations or a play on words, but the origins of the more unusual ones cannot be ascertained.

DAISY Bell – perhaps from the name of the song 'Daisy, Daisy' ('… give me your answer, do …'), or from a cow's bell.

WINDY Gale

PIGGY May

TOMMY Thomas

WIGGY Bennett

BETSY Gay

DUSTY Miller

TOPSY Turner – possibly related to the term topsy-turvy.

CHARLIE Beresford – after Admiral Lord Charlie Beresford (1846–1919).

TOSH Gilbert

PONY Moore – after George Washington 'Pony' Moore (1820–1909) who was, as well as running various music halls, well known for his love of betting, and allegedly always bet in 'ponies' (betting slang for a sum of £25).

GUY Vaughan

DOLLY Gray – from the song 'Goodbye Dolly Gray', a famous marching song from both the Boer War and First World War.

SPUD Murphy – a word play; Murphy being a common Irish surname and 'spud' a reference to the Irish Potato Famine.

HOOKEY Walker – probably derived from Mr John Walker, an outdoor clerk of Messrs Longman Clementini & Co., formerly of Cheapside, in the early nineteenth century. He was allegedly an unpleasant man, and would invent bad reports of his co-workers. He was noted for his hook nose.

JOHNNY Bone

JIMMY Green

CHARLIE Noble

NELLY Wallace

RAJAH Brookes

CHATS Harris

NOSEY Parker

SHARKEY Ward – after the nickname of John Ward (c. 1553–1622), an English sea captain turned Barbary Corsair (when he became known as Yusuf Rais). The origin of his nickname 'sharkey' is unknown.

GINGER Casey
GRANNY Henderson
WHACKER Payne
BANJO West
NOBBY Clark – this interesting name comes from the social climbers of the Industrial Revolution. As commoners became wealthy, people changed the spelling of their names. Smith became Smythe, Brown became Browne and Clark became Clarke. The less wealthy members of the family who became ostracised called their snooty relatives the nobs or the Nobby Clarks (from 'nobility').
NOBBY/NOSHER Hewitt
JACK Shepherd
KNOCKER White
JUMPER Collins
COSHER Hinds
JUMPER Short
TUG Wilson – from the nickname of First Sea Lord and Admiral of the Fleet, Sir Arthur 'Tug' Kynvet Wilson (1842–1921).
HAPPY Day
GIBLEY Howe
FROSTY Snow
TIMBER Wood
BANDY Evans
FLAPPER Hughes
RUSTY Steel
SLINGER Woods
NOBBY Ewart
BOGIE Knight
SPIKE Sullivan
SHINER Wright
FLORRIE Ford – named after the Australian-born music-hall singer, most famous for the song 'Down at the Old Bull and Bush'.
DODGER Long – as in dodge along, i.e. run along.
BUCK Taylor
BRIGHAM Young – after the leader of the Mormons during the migration to Utah.
HARRY Freeman
PINCHER Martin – from the nickname of Admiral Sir W. F. Martin (1801–95), who was renowned for being a strict disciplinarian and did not

hesitate to 'pinch' ratings for minor offences.
SNIP Taylor
Source: Covey Crump

There are new nicknames being created all the time, where the inspiration ranges from serial killers (FRED West), to cars (MINI Cooper), to British footballing heroes (ALF Ramsey, JOE Royle, STANLEY Matthews).

Bilge water/bilge rat

On land many people use the words 'bilge' or 'bilge water' when referring to something they deem foul, obnoxious or absolute rubbish. In 2001 European Commission Vice President Neil Kinnock commented on the way British newspapers react to stories and rumours emanating from Brussels:

> *I am weary of it most of all not because of the damage inflicted on the EU by this – that doesn't matter all that much. What does matter is the perpetual disservice done to the readers of several British newspapers ... who continually pump out this bilge which simply doesn't have a basis and can only add to feelings of bewilderment or antagonism amongst British people.*

On board a ship the bilge is the lowest part of the hull, the area directly above the keel. The word seems to derive from the French *bouge* – referring to the pronounced curvature of the hull under the waterline, i.e. the bulge. This was where the ballast was stowed to provide the ship with a low centre of gravity. In a sailing ship this would be pig iron (brittle iron that had little use ashore) covered with shingle. In addition, all the ships' stores were stowed in this area either on platforms or in casks resting on the shingle. Due to the effects of gravity any water that entered the ship would

eventually work down and collect in the hold becoming bilge water. As gravity also affects other types of liquid on board ship, bilge water could contain a heady mix of sweat, oil, blood, faeces, urine, saliva, pitch, semen – not a particularly pleasant concoction. It was not unknown for bilge water to produce foul, noxious gases; in some instances sailors actually suffocated from its effects. One visitor to the US ship *Hornet* remarked, 'great quantities of mud and other filth were taken out of her hold … The bilge water, and smell from the hold in this vessel were exceedingly unpleasant'. Bilge water was bad enough in wooden ships but it could corrode iron, a major problem for the iron-hulled vessels of the nineteenth century.

It is interesting that in the oldest sea ballad known, 'The Pilgrims Sea Voyage', dating from 1430, the problems of foul bilge water were evident:

A sak of strawe were there ryght good
Ffor some must lyg theym in theyr hood:
I had as lefe be in the wood,
Without mete or drynk.

For when that we shall go to bedde,
The pumpe is nygh our beddes hede;
A man were as good to be dede
As smell therof the stynk!

Bilge water could be pumped out but due to rain and storms there would always be a quantity in a sailing man-of-war. On HMS *Pegasus* in 1787, 'Whenever there are 16 inches of water in the hold, the First Lieutenant at anchor and the officer of the watch at sea, are to have the ship pumped out'. While this might act as a short-term solution, the only way to completely remove foul bilge water on a sailing warship was to cleanse and rinse the pig iron and shingle ballast. If disease broke out among the crew one of the options open to a captain was to completely remove the ballast and replace it with fresh. Hit by an epidemic in 1790 HMS *Elephant* had 316 tons of ballast removed allowing the ship to be fumigated with tobacco and washed out with vinegar before fresh shingle was taken onboard. Even today bilge water remains a problem for ships, particularly when mixed with petroleum or oil, as the parts need to be separated before it can be disposed of. Dumping bilge water overboard is illegal, as the crew of MSC *Trinidad* found out in May 2008 when detained by Canadian authorities for allegedly dumping up to 30 tons of bilge water off the coast of Newfoundland.

'**Bilge rat**' is an insulting term beloved by writers of pirate fiction. The dark, dank and musty conditions in the hold were the favoured habitat of rats that would breed in the hold. The term then came to be used for members of the crew who work in the bowels of the ship and hence near the bilge rats. In the Royal Navy the term was sometimes used to describe stokers. These were originally the men who continually shovelled coal into the boilers of steam-powered warships, working below the waterline in hot sweaty conditions, covered from head to foot in coal dust.

Stinkpot

Stinkpot is a derisive term suggesting that a person might smell bad, perhaps due to poor personal hygiene. For instance, from *A Portrait of the Artist as a Young Man* by James Joyce, "'Go away from here," he said rudely. "Go away, you stinkpot. And you are a stinkpot". The origin has nothing to do with the Common Musk Turtle (*Sternotherus odoratus*), commonly known as the stinkpot turtle, a native of North America which can emit a foul, musky smell to ward off predators.

A stinkpot was an explosive weapon used at sea during the Classical and Medieval periods until superseded by cannon. A stinkpot comprised a pottery jar filled with combustible material such as gunpowder, or a noxious material such as lime. Combustion came from a rudimentary fuse. Stinkpots could either be loaded onto a catapult and fired, or thrown from the deck of a ship. They were primarily anti-personnel weapons, perhaps used to disrupt, disorganise and terrify rather than inflict casualties. Due to the nature of their contents, especially if containing sulphur, in addition to the resultant conflagration they would also emit a noxious stench. They were an early type of grenade.

Perhaps the most famous use of such infernal devices was by the notorious pirate Edward Teach, more commonly known as Blackbeard. Captain Charles Johnson, in his book *A General History of the Robberies and Murders of the Most Notorious Pirates* describes it thus:

> *Captain Teach's men threw in several new fashioned sort of grenades, viz. case bottles filled with powder and small shot, slugs and pieces of lead or iron, with a quick match in the mouth of it, which being lighted without side, presently runs into the bottle to the powder, and as it is instantly thrown on board, generally does great execution, besides putting all the crew into a confusion.*

A selection of sea words

Joiner
Nothing to do with a man's woodworking skills, but the sailors' slang for a person joining a drinking party who partakes of other peoples drinks rounds but departs before it is his turn to pay for a round.

Tosser
The rather bizarre occasional slang name for a signal rating.

Ullage
The remnants of useless grog in a cask, and hence is used in relation to a useless or stupid rating.

Piss flap
The buttoned flap on the front of a sailor's trousers.

Pig's ear
Used by the men on watch to answer a call of nature, this was an upper deck urinal in the shape of a pig's ear. The action of using this device was called 'seeing Auntie'.

C.U.N.T.
In the US Navy a Civilian Under Naval Training.

Gobbler's gulch
The rather tender area of a woman's leg between the top of a stocking and a suspender belt.

Cock and arse party
The sailor's slang for an officer's cocktail party.

Tuna boat
In the US Navy a non-combat vessel crewed mainly by female sailors.

Bootnecks/Jollies/Royals/Turkey/Leathernecks
British ailors' nicknames for Royal Marines.

Jarhead
Nickname for US Marine, after their distinctive haircuts (or possibly because they are thought of as being thick headed).

Sprog
Any new or junior member of a ship's crew.

Jewing bag
A small bag in which a sailor kept his sewing kit, named because many tailors were Jewish.

Enswine
Term used when referring to an ensign rating.

Fleet meat
US Navy term for promiscuous female sailors.

Cum dumpster
Female ashore used by sailors for a quickie.

Buffer
In the Royal Navy the boastwain's chief mate; according to legend it stands for Big Ugly Fat Fucker Easily Replaced.

Double breasted matelot
Royal Navy slang for a female sailor.

Free traders
French knickers, very loose fitting round the leg and crotch they allow easy access.

Black-hand gang
Old slang for stokers and other engine-room crew derived from their being covered in coal dust.

Slice of black ham
Politically incorrect slang for visiting an African prostitute.

Jockanese
The distinct language spoken by Scottish sailors.

ARAB
Royal Navy slang relating to British army officers: Arrogant Regular Army Bastard.

Knacker crackers
Rather fulsome and sturdy thighs as possessed by a percentage of female sailors.

Flashing up a lawn mower
An attempt to hook up with another sailor's wife or girlfriend while he is away at sea.

Out of watch
Sex with a female who is not one's wife or girlfriend.

A-Farts
Another case of an amusing acronym, this is US Navy slang for the Armed Forces Radio & Television Service.

Split-arse matelot
Female rating sometimes shortened to splits. A split-arsed mechanic is a less than attractive female sailor.

Scab lifter
Any member of the Medical profession onboard ship, in the US Navy is sometimes called a Pecker Checker or Dick Doc.

Airy fairy
Sailor slang for Fleet Air Arm personnel. In the US Navy a naval aviator is known as an Airdale or a Brownshoe.

Gronk
United States naval slang for an ugly woman, pictures of such conquests are displayed in the mess on a Gronk board.

Abu Dhabi/Hajji pop
Canned drinks with Arabic lettering, found on board ship when serving in the Persian Gulf.

Base bunny
Loose (and in some cases, crazed) women who hang round US Navy bases looking for sailors. Before *Fatal Attraction* inspired the term 'bunny boiler', from which this phrase derives, such ladies were called 'sea hags'.

Nigerian lager
A pint of Guinness, so called as Nigeria not only boasts the largest Guinness Brewery (in Lagos) but the country is also the world's number one consumer of the black stuff.

Showerbabies
Semen left in showers by sailors who have been waxing the dolphin.

Smiles
This game is played by sailors enjoying a run ashore in a foreign port. While playing cards, under the table a prostitute performs oral sex on all the players. The first to crack a smile buys the beers.

Pig of the port
Award given to the sailor who picks up the ugliest woman.

Refresher training
A specific time set aside while heading for home port, during which the crew watch pornographic films.

F.U.P.A.
Used to describe an overweight female sailor whose tight-fitting trousers produce a bulge thereby giving a 'Fat Upper Pussy Area', can also be called a B.U.F.: 'Butt up Front'.

Kytai
Transvestite.

B.O.S.N.I.A.
United States naval slang referring to anyone equipped with a Big Ol' Standard Navy Issue Ass.

Lower deck lawyer
Any sailor who pontificates about regulations – usually when other sailors are bending them.

10

FLOTSAM AND JETSAM

There are many other words and phrases used by sailors that do not fit into the previous chapters. From place nicknames to 'tomfoolery', messages in bottles to the 'Jolly Roger' pirate flag, this chapter contains a smorgasbord of slang.

Flotsam and jetsam

Walk along any beach and you will see a variety of items washed ashore by the sea. This is flotsam and jetsam – and there is a lot of it about. The huge container ships that carry cargoes around the globe lose around 10,000 containers each year. Sometimes they break open, spilling their contents into the sea. This can include everything from plastic bottles to false legs, rubber ducks to training shoes. Carried by the tide such goods eventually find their way ashore, leading to some bizarre events. The beach at Frisco, North Carolina, was littered with bags of Doritos in 2006. Branscombe Beach in Devon hit the news in 2007 when the MSC *Napoli* beached offshore spilling hundreds of containers which washed up along the south coast of England. This prompted entrepreneurial locals to engage in the time-honoured tradition of scavenging; items taken included, around 50 BMW motorcycles, casks of wine, shoes, bibles, cosmetics and car parts. Things started to get out of hand and the police were forced to enact legislation not used for a century to try to reclaim goods. Most people did not realise that under the 1995 Merchant Shipping Act, failure to declare salvaged goods was an offence comparable to theft, as the goods still belong to their original owners. Moreover, some of the containers contained hazardous material.

For many this brought back images of a nineteenth-century phenomenon: wrecking. Throughout history, people living along particularly dangerous coastlines have seen wrecked ships and washed-up goods as fair game. From the Florida Keys to the Devon and Cornwall coasts, wreckers have plundered ships for valuable goods. The wreckers gained notoriety because of an ancient law which declared that if no one survived the wreck then the owners had no claim to it. Stories circulated of false lights hoisted on dark stormy nights, luring ships to be dashed to pieces on submerged rocks. Any survivors would be quickly despatched allowing the wreckers to claim possession of the goods.

At first it seems there is little difference between flotsam and jetsam, yet they are two distinctly different entities.

Flotsam are goods that find their way into the sea either when a ship sinks or lost overboard. Today it also includes all of the varied flora and fauna that wash up ashore, such as driftwood and seaweed.

Jetsam is all the things intentionally thrown overboard, perhaps to lighten the ship; dumping rubbish or getting rid of prohibited goods.

To these must be added a third category, **Ligan**: items thrown into the sea but with a buoy or marker for retrieval at a later time.

Perhaps the most famous item of jetsam is the 'message in a bottle'. This has long been a staple ingredient in stories of mariners marooned on desert islands. It also provided inspiration for Sting to write the song 'Message In a Bottle', which became the Police's first UK Number 1 in 1979. While many bottles washed up ashore later prove to be hoaxes, there are some cases in which the truth is stranger than fiction. In May 2005, CNN reported that 88 Peruvians and Ecuadorians had been rescued after drifting for three days off the coast of Costa Rica. They had paid people-traffickers to take them to the United States, but when the boat started taking on water the traffickers absconded leaving the migrants to fend for themselves. Upon seeing long fishing lines in the water, one of the migrants came up with a plan to write a message in a bottle and attached it to the lines. Upon drawing in her nets the crew of the fishing boat, the *Rey de Reyes*, found the message, alerted the authorities and the migrants were rescued.

Ring out the old, ring in the new

> Ring out the old, ring in the new,
> Ring, happy bells, across the snow:
> The year is going, let him go;
> Ring out the false, ring in the true.
>> Ring Out, Wild Bells by Alfred Tennyson

Ashore this phrase is used liberally for describing epoch-marking events. For example when the British Labour Party swept to power in May 1997 columnist William Rees-Mogg 'found Tennyson running through my mind as the results came in' and was suitably moved to quote from Tennyson's poem above. It is also used in reference to the passing of an old year and the arrival of a new one.

In Chapter 4 we looked at how the naval day is organised into watches, and that the passage of time was marked by the striking of bells. So it is no surprise that the monotonous routine of this system was broken on one day, 31 December, New Year's Eve. As Captain, later Admiral, Albert Hastings Markham, explains in his narrative of the Arctic expedition of 1875 in HMS *Alert*: 'It is generally the custom in the navy to strike the bell sixteen times at midnight on New Year's eve: eight bells for the old year and eight bells for the new'. On board the battleship HMS *Canopus* New Year's Eve 1914 was celebrated by the officers, one sailor wryly recounted, 'we can hear our officers singing and dancing and ringing the old Year out, at 12 o'clock they all came on the Quarter Deck all the worst for drink'.

Striking sixteen bells is a tradition still enacted in today's Royal Navy where the youngest officer on board has the honour of striking the bell. In the past this was a rather dubious honour because the ceremony was seen as an ideal time for a bit of tomfoolery by mischievous ratings. It was not uncommon for the rating to find the bell-rope covered with marmalade or some other sticky substance. It is also alleged that on some ships the bell-rope was wired up to an electric current to give out a mild charge to the shocked young officer.

To fudge

To 'fudge' is to fake or cheat at something. For example, the *New York Times* of 2 February 2006 ran a story entitled, 'Ex-Executive Says Enron Fudged Data'. The article stated:

> *In surprising testimony on Wednesday, Enron's former head of investor relations [Mark E. Koenig] said that the company fudged its quarterly earnings and repeatedly lied to Wall Street about the true condition of its troubled broadband services division to keep its stock price soaring.*

Certainly most people would agree that the Enron case is a prime example of a company seemingly 'fudging' the books to mislead analysts and investors.

The origin of the term does not stem from the sweet, soft buttermilk candy called fudge, so called, at least the story goes, because it came from a botched batch of caramel. The word 'fudge' was in use well before this tale, which dates from 1886. In fact 'fudge' seemingly dates back to the seventeenth century and the diary of Samuel Pepys. Contained in Pepys's acerbic writings on London life are his frustrations at a man called Captain Fudge. After describing a most entertaining tiff with his wife ('she had the cunning to cry a great while, and talk and blubber') on Sunday, 12 June 1664, Pepys was,

> *... troubled in my mind also about the knavery and neglect of Captain Fudge and Taylor, who were to have had their ship for Tangier ready by Thursday last, and now the men by a mistake are come on board, and not any master or man or boy of the ship's company on board with them when we came by her side this afternoon, and also received a letter from Mr. Coventry this day in complaint of it.*

Determined to find out what was going on, next day Pepys, 'called upon Fudge, whom I found like a lying rogue unready to go on board'. So this Captain Fudge had been telling lies to Pepys, who was at that time Clerk of the Acts to the Navy Board. Even worse, the following year Fudge was in command of the Merchant ship *Black Eagle* with a cargo of Quakers for Transportation to the West Indies. Due to his prevarication and general ineffectiveness plague infested the ship killing eight of the crew and nineteen prisoners, the crew mutinied and Fudge was arrested as a debtor. In 1841 Isaac Disraeli quoted from a pamphlet entitled 'Remarks on the Navy' dating from 1700. The author of the pamphlet declared:

> *There was, sir, in our time, one Captain Fudge ... who upon his return from a voyage, how ill-fraught soever his ship was, always brought home his owners a good cargo of lies; so much that now, aboard ship, the sailors, when they hear a great lie told, cry out, 'You fudge it!'*

The Jolly Roger

> *... the anchorage, under lee of Skeleton Island, lay still and leaden as when we first entered it. The* Hispaniola *... was exactly portrayed from the truck to the waterline, the Jolly Roger hanging from her peak.*
>
> *Treasure Island* by Robert Louis Stevenson

'The Jolly Roger' is a strange name for a flag. Most people think of it as comprised a skull and crossbones, but many pirates customised the overall

look and feel of the classic skull and crossbones design. Versions of it have appeared in Pirate movies for decades, right up to the recent *Pirates of the Caribbean* trilogy. In fact, Captain Jack Sparrow's ship, the *Black Pearl*, is seen flying a real pirate flag. The design, a skull with crossed swords, belonged to 'Calico' Jack Rackham, a notorious pirate executed in Jamaica in 1720 and known to history for his love of garish clothes and for having two female pirates in his crew. The flag of another pirate, 'Black' Bart Roberts, appears in *Pirates of the Caribbean: At World's End*. In fact Roberts had at least two flags; one depicted him and the figure of death holding an hourglass. Another, made of black silk, had:

> … *a death in it, with an hour-glass in one hand, and cross bones in the other, a dart by it, and underneath a heart dropping three drops of blood.*

The use of the Jolly Roger was certainly an example of psychological warfare: pirates wanted to capture ships, not sink them, so flying a distinctive flag was designed to strike terror into the hearts of the target. By flying the Jolly Roger the pirates were offering quarter in the hope the victim would surrender without a fight. If they did not take this opportunity they could expect no mercy, the Jolly Roger was run down and a blood-red flag hoisted in its stead. The name 'Jolly Roger' is certainly contemporary to the end of the Golden Age of Piracy, as it appears in *A General History of the Pyrates* by Captain Charles Johnson first published in 1724. It could be derived from an old name for the Devil: 'Old Roger'.

The Jolly Roger is still used today, not by pirates, but by the Royal Navy. In September 1914 Lieutenant-Commander Max Horton in *E9* became the first

Royal Navy submarine commander to sink an enemy vessel, the German cruiser *Hela*. Returning to Harwich Horton hoisted a Jolly Roger, thereby starting a famous tradition. It continued during the Second World War; in 1940 Stoker Sydney Hart remarked, 'through hazy eyes I spotted *Truant* tying up to a buoy in the Creek, with two more bars on her jolly Roger, as indication that she had sunk two fresh ships on her latest patrol'. After the Falklands War, HMS *Conqueror* returned to her base at Faslane flying the flag as a mark of her 'kill', the Argentine ship *General Belgrano*.

With the recent craze for all things pirate-related across the UK, many individuals have been caught out flying the Jolly Roger. In May 2008 one resident of Ashstead, Surrey, became only the latest individuals to be threatened with legal proceedings by his local council for flying a Jolly Roger outside his house as part of a pirate-themed birthday party for his daughter. The council deemed the flag constituted a breach of advertising regulations under the Outdoor Advertisements & Signs Regulations.

Guzz

Guzz is the traditional naval name for Plymouth, specifically the naval base of Devonport. There are several possible explanations for the term, none of which are satisfactorily conclusive. Covey Crump sticks with the original interpretation that it comes from the sailing navy where sailors would guzzle up their food and drink upon returning to the port. Another explanation points to GUZZ as the First World War radio call-sign for Devonport, but there is little evidence for this. Godfrey Dykes, who has investigated the matter at some length, speculates that in the West Country dialect an oarsman could have been called to 'gozell ouer' – sailors would have been rowed ashore from ships moored in the River Hamoaze. It is highly likely that this is one term that will remain something of a mystery.

Pompey

This is the sailors' name for Portsmouth. It is also the nickname of Portsmouth Football Club. Again, as with 'Guzz', there are several less than conclusive theories as to the origin. According to naval folklore drunken sailors would habitually get lost ashore and ask directions to 'Portsmouth Point' where a number of popular ale houses were located. In such a drunken state the sailors would mispronounce 'Portsmouth

Point' as 'pompey'. Another possibility is the scaling of the Pompey's Pillar in Egypt by some sailors from Portsmouth in 1781. Upon reaching the top they toasted 'Pompey' and hence became knows as 'Pompey Boys'. Yet another theory relates to the French ship *Pompée* handed over to the British by the Anti-French Revolution forces in Toulon during 1794. Taken into the Royal Navy, this ship ended her days as a prison hulk in Portsmouth Harbour.

Sheer Nasty

Old naval slang for the Medway town of Sheerness. After the Dutch raided the Medway in 1667, Samuel Pepys ordered a naval dockyard to be built at Sheerness in 1669. Sheerness was often called 'The last place God made' by sailors. The origins of the term are obscured, but one could speculate a play on words.

Fairway

Whack down the fairway
It went smack down the fairway
Then it started to slice just a smidge off line
It headed for two but it bounced off nine
My caddie says long as you're still in the state you're okay
Yes it went straight down the middle quite a ways
Bing Crosby

What is the connection between Bing Crosby's lament for a lost golf ball and nautical slang? The clear open part of a golf hole between the tee and the green is known as a 'fairway'. It's where you want your ball to land when you tee off, avoiding all hazards and leaving a clear shot into the green. Well, 'fairway' is also a word frequently applied in nautical law. It means the clear passage, i.e. devoid of hazards and obstacles, into a port, harbour or river. The game of golf is itself ancient, perhaps dating to the twelfth century with the first recorded game occurring in 1456 at Bruntsfield Links, Edinburgh. Although this predates the earliest use of the word 'fairway' in relation to navigation, that occurring in 1584, the term does not seem to have been used in golfing terms until the twentieth century.

A navigable fairway was defined by J. Bruce as, 'Wherever there is an open navigable passage used by vessels proceeding up and down a river or channel, that may be said to be a fairway'. To which Smyth adds, 'Also, when the proper course is gained out of a channel'. In Robert Louis Stevenson's *Treasure Island* the narrator, Jim Hawkins, declares,

> *'By good fortune, paddle as I pleased, the tide was still sweeping me down; and there lay the* Hispaniola *right in the fairway, hardly to be missed ...'*

In following the fairway a sailor is following a safe and navigable passage, in much the same way that a golfer wishes to follow the fairway on a golf course. If the latter does not, all that might happen is that he ends up in a bunker, the rough, or like Bing, loses his ball. For the sailor not keeping to the fairway could have disastrous consequences; submerged sandbanks, reefs and other obstacles could wreck his ship.

Naturally, in time of war fairways play a key strategic role. In April 1918 the Royal Navy launched an operation to block the port of Ostend and the inland port of Bruges. If successful the operation would have prevented the Germans using the ports as bases for their U-boats. The plan failed due to a wily German commander moving the only navigation buoy marking the fairway to lure the British attack onto submerged sandbanks. In reporting the operation *The New York Times* of 25 April 1918 was unrealistically optimistic, '20 Yards of Mole Blown Up; Ostend Fairway is Blocked'.

Skylarking

In a previous chapter we looked at how the skyscraper sail gave its name to the tall buildings that shot up in North American cities during the late-nineteenth and early twentieth centuries. Here we can look at a word that has had very common usage ashore, for to 'skylark' is to fool about, to play. More often than not the 'sky' part is dropped from the phrase leaving us with the colloquial 'lark' or 'larking'. 'Lark' comes from the old English word '*lac*', meaning to play. In the world of Aves, the skylark is a small brownish bird, noted for its singing while in flight, thus appearing most playful.

At sea, skylarking was the procedure of rapidly climbing the rigging to the mast heads, then even more rapidly descending to the deck by sliding down the royal-stays or back-stays. The Admiralty considered such exercises an essential part of teaching young sailors the skills necessary for their future careers, ships' captains were:

> *... to take care that they be practised in going frequently every day up and down the shrouds and employed on all kinds of work which are to be*

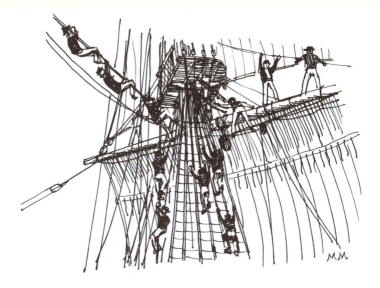

created in purpose for them both to keep them in action and to teach them the duty of seamen …

Of course there was the added incentive that ships should take pride in trying to outdo each other in skill and speed. Exercising the hands, both young and experienced, in this way was an essential part of working up a ship's crew ready for a long voyage. For those young gentlemen who joined the navy as midshipmen and were, hopefully, destined for the quarterdeck, working among the topmen was essential to grasp the fundamentals of seamanship.

With ships spending long hours at sea there was plenty of opportunity not only to hone the skills of the crew but to prevent the onset of boredom with the hands being piped to 'dance and skylark'. With the large number of boys and young adults on board a ship there was plenty of opportunity for anything from good-natured horseplay to downright vicious bullying. By the nineteenth century 'skylarking' had become more formalised with a string of boys following their leader through the rigging of a ship, the term then started to be used ashore for any type of 'frolicsome mischief'.

This latter usage appears in two nineteenth-century classics. In his *Voyage of the Beagle*, Charles Darwin recalled how one member of the crew was well ,liked, but another crew member, Jemmy, 'did not at all like this, and used to say, with rather a contemptuous twist of his head, ' "too much skylark"'. In *Moby Dick* Herman Melville describes a conversation between Stubb, second mate of the *Pequod* and Flask, the third mate:

'Why, do ye see, the old man is hard bent after that White Whale, and the devil there is trying to come round him, and get him to swap away his silver watch, or his soul, or something of that sort, and then he'll surrender Moby Dick.'

'Pooh! Stubb, you are skylarking; how can Fedallah [Ahab's Parsi harpooner] do that?'

'I don't know, Flask, but the devil is a curious chap, and a wicked one, I tell ye.'

Crossed the line

> 'You, my friend, have crossed the line that divides man and bum. You are now a bum.'
>
> Jerry Seinfeld to George Costanza, 'The Gymnast', *Seinfeld*

Ashore, 'crossing the line' can mean two things. There is traversing a geographical line, for instance crossing a border, a finish line or a railway line. Then there is a metaphorical meaning; when someone is said to have 'crossed the line', they have taken a momentous step. Sometimes it is used to describe a person who has overstepped a mark, engaging in some outrageous behaviour that is not deemed acceptable by their peers or perhaps acting in a foolhardy manner. Once the line has been crossed there is no going back. Reporting on the news that the US Government had been keeping its citizens under surveillance through the use of phone records *The Times* of 12 May 2006 declared, 'Bush may have crossed the line by tracking every US phone call'.

On board ship, 'crossing the line' is to cross the equatorial line from one hemisphere to the other. All the sailors that have previously crossed the equatorial line are called 'Trusty Shellbacks' and must initiate those sailors who are crossing for the first time, known as 'Slimy Pollywogs'. The ceremony itself takes place over two days and is a chaotic mix of bizarre rituals and punishments, all carried out in a number of fetching costumes. On the eve of the line crossing the Pollywogs revolt and can play any number of pranks on the Shellbacks. Retribution comes the next day when King Neptune, Queen Amphitrite and their court take over the ship. On board HMS *Boadicea* in 1943 an eyewitness recorded: 'The costumes made a brave show in the tropical sunlight, that of His Majesty doing much to enhance his natural dignity, and his Queen's tasteful selection of apparel for the occasion made many a matelot's heart beat a little faster'. On the USS *Pintado*, Corwin Meridenhall noted: 'The Queen wore an outfit of women's underwear that was found in a bale of cleaning rags. She looked quite curvy, with balls of twine in the bra'.

Once Neptune and his court have taken their rightful places on the quarterdeck, honours are bestowed on those deserving them. On *Boadicea* Lieutenant Commander Brodrick was invested with 'Order of the Ship Handler First Class – Without Tugs and Pilot's Certificate' for his ability to 'steer a straight course for Watney's Brewery' amongst other achievements, while the Engineer Officer was presented with the 'Order of the Rusty Kipper'. After the awards it is time for the Pollywogs to be punished with miscreants presented to the Court, various offences read out, judgement given and punishment administered by Neptune's bears. An example from *Boadicea* will provide a suitable illustration:

Surgeon-Lieutenant Cliff
Charge: Did cause to be brought to the Bay of Sickness for vile potions and injections; was guilty of being the worst Chess player on the ship, and did spread 'Buzz'. Did display wicked instruments when loyal subjects reported for inoculation.
Judgement: To return his Pork Sword, have his scalpel removed, his Arkin-in-set to be abandoned; pulse removed, blood pressure revved up, scrotum painted with silver nitrate, and what is left to be thrown to the bears.

With judgement passed the offender would be administered some foul concoction – on *Pintado* this was 'a piece of cake made with soap powder, garlic, salt, and other awful-tasting things'. The Pollywog was then passed over to the Barber to have shaving foam, grease, paint, oil, syrup or some other substance liberally applied then have it shaved off before being ducked in a bath. Pollywogs can be herded by the Shellbacks and Bears, who are sometimes equipped with lengths of hosepipe with which to provide

'encouragement', to complete a series of tasks, such as wearing clothes inside out, climbing ladders onto makeshift chutes and sliding down into baths of dubious liquids, walking on hands and knees and so on. Upon successful completion of the ceremony the Pollywogs are no more, instead they have graduated to Shellback status. On *Boadicea* the new Shellbacks seized the Court and ensured that they too received a good ducking. Drinks are usually served before Neptune and his Court 'return to the watery depths' to await the arrival of the next ship to cross the line.

Gung-ho

> *In 'Moby Dick Rehearsed' … Gung-ho actors bring everything vividly to life with no more than some crates and ladders for scenery. At times the entire theater feels like a ship at sea: as the actors sway in unison to indicate the motion of the waves, you may find yourself swaying as well.*
>
> Neil Genzlinger, *The New York Times*, 10 May 2008

Many of the words and phrases in this book originated in the eighteenth and nineteenth centuries, but 'gung-ho' is a relatively recent addition to the sailor's vocabulary, dating to the Second World War. To be 'gung-ho' is to be eager, enthusiastic and perhaps even a little overzealous. The use of the phrase has developed from this original meaning to include those who might bend the rules to get what they want or do something without thinking of the consequences, maybe even putting others at risk by their actions.

The word comes from Mandarin Chinese. In 1937 Japan invaded China, thereby sparking the Second Sino-Japanese War that would last until 1945. As part of a strategy of resistance the Chinese Government set up the Chinese Industrial Cooperative Association to organise work for refugees fleeing the combat zones and to provide logistical support to the Chinese troops fighting the Japanese. Behind the movement was a New Zealander called Rewi Alley, who coined the organisation's motto (mottos are an integral part of communist ideology and Alley was sympathetic to their cause) '*Gōnghé*' meaning 'to work together'. It was soon picked up by China's National Revolutionary Army.

In China at this time, acting as an observer, was Evans Carlson of the US Marine Corps. Carlson visited Communist HQ's, travelled with the Eighth Route Army, lived with communist guerrillas and witnessed at first hand the tactics the Japanese would use so effectively during the Second World War.

Carlson left China in 1938 and resigned his commission the following year. In 1941, increasingly concerned about Japanese intentions, he rejoined the USMC and the following year led the Second Marine Raider Battalion. Carlson used the knowledge he had acquired during his time in China; he even used communist ideals and methods including the 'work together' ethos to solve problems which Carlson called 'gung ho' meetings. The phrase caught on with his unit, nicknamed 'Carlson's Raiders', and then spread to the USMC. Carlson led his men in an amphibious attack on Japanese positions at Makin Island in August 1942. This operation formed the plot basis for a film the following year called *Gung Ho! The Story of Carlson's Makin Island Raiders* with Randolph Scott playing a fictional Lieutenant Colonel Throwald based on Carlson. The film was a success and the phrase 'gung-ho' entered American popular culture.

Tombola

Tombola is a game of chance popular at village fêtes, Women's Institute meetings, sporting club dinners and a whole host of other gatherings. In the UK most people will have played a variant of the tombola: the National Lotto. The British Army also play the game where it is called 'Housey-Housey', while the popular game of Bingo is a variant of the original.

The game itself comes from southern Italy, the word 'tombola' is derived from *tombolare* meaning 'tumble, fall upside down'. The Royal Navy first encountered this game of chance in Malta around 1880; the inhabitants of that small island were obsessed with the game. Gambling was officially forbidden on Royal Navy ships (though card schools often took place out of the way of prying eyes) excepting the tombola, which was run in a coordinated fashion.

Numbered tickets come in brightly coloured strips with the purchaser taking one half of the ticket while the other is usually put in a container. The classic tombola uses a special drum which can be turned, thereby causing the tickets to tumble around ensuring that those drawing the tickets do so in a fair manner. In other versions, hats, cake tins and cardboard boxes have all been used to draw winning tickets.

Another version, from which modern bingo is derived, uses cards with numbers printed on them which can be marked off when the relevant number is drawn. The first to complete a line can win a prize, with a larger prize for completing the whole card, known as 'house'. Many of the numbers have their own nicknames, some of those used afloat include:

1. Kelly's eye
6. Spot below – number 6 has a dot beneath it to prevent confusion with 9.
9. Doctor's Joy – cure-all pill dispensed by the ship's doctor.
11. Legs eleven
13. Lucky for some
17. Old Ireland – St Patrick's Day, 17 March.
20. One score
21. Bang bang bang – 21 Gun Salute.
22. PC Parker
45. Half way
59. The Brighton Line – London Brighton South Coast line fare to London was 5/9d.
62. To Waterloo – London and South Western line fare from Portsmouth to London was 6/2d.
66. Clicketty-click
69. Whichever way you look at it
89. All but, Maltese goat
90. Top of the house
Source: Covey Crump

Ships in the Royal Navy still organise tombola, sometimes on a weekly basis with proceeds going to charitable causes.

Sailor's Hornpipe

The Sailor's Hornpipe is a traditional seafaring dance accompanied by music. Most people will be familiar with the tune from one of two sources. Sir Henry Wood included it in his *Fantasia on British Sea Songs* composed in 1905 to mark the centenary of the Battle of Trafalgar and which is traditionally performed at the BBC's Last Night of the Proms. The tune also appears at the very end of Mike Oldfield's ground-breaking 1973 album *Tubular Bells*, increasing in speed to almost demonic proportions. The hornpipe itself was a member of the woodwind family, composed of an animal horn with spaced holes, a reed, and either played with a bag or by mouth. While this could have been the original instrument to accompany the dance, a tin whistle was common until superseded by the accordion in the nineteenth century and which would be the most familiar to a modern audience.

The tune of the 'Sailor's Hornpipe' dates to at least the eighteenth century, though an earlier composition date is extremely likely. In the fourteenth century Chaucer makes reference to hornpipes being danced in Cornwall, a region noted for its seafaring heritage, 'Controve he welde and foule fayla with hornepypes of cornewayle'. In the fifteenth century a 'mystery' stage play concluded with 'mynstrellys on hornpipe'. In the seventeenth century Pepys references the 'Jig of the Ship' but it was not until the late eighteenth century that the music was actually put to paper as the 'College Hornpipe'.

The dance that traditionally accompanies the tune is highly significant for it replicates the various tasks (hauling, rowing, climbing) that a sailor would complete as part of his daily duties on board ship. Dancing played a big role in the sailor's life as it provided entertainment and social intercourse, and was good for morale. In the confined spaces on board ship, which limited extravagant manoeuvres, the hornpipe developed as a solo dance. Able seamen working aloft would get plenty exercise climbing up and down rigging, it was common for hands to be piped to 'dance and skylark' with the younger members playing in the rigging, landsmen and other **idlers** who would not work aloft, danced for exercise. Dancing was a nightly event on board Admiral Edward Boscawen's flagship the 90-gun *Namur* in 1755 as she sailed west across the Atlantic and Captain James Cook regularly exercised his crews by having them dance the hornpipe.

APPENDIX

A Run Ashore: Images of the Sailor in Popular Culture

From saucy seaside postcards to drama, from Hollywood blockbusters to pop songs, people ashore have often made judgements about the sailor's life. Two examples will show how deeply embedded the sailor is in our culture. The sublimely gruff and realistic Boatswain in Shakespeare's *The Tempest* is a good old seadog, who knows his business. On the other hand, there is the lighthearted image of Gene Kelly and Frank Sinatra dancing their way round the sights while singing 'New York, New York, it's a wonderful town' in *On the Town*. This essay is by no means an exhaustive study of all the ways sailors have been represented ashore; consider it more of a guide on where to look.

In Jane Austen's *Persuasion*, published in 1818 after her death the previous year, the relationship between Captain Wentworth RN and Anne Elliot is at the centre of the plot. Austen's portrayal of the value of appearances and money over true love is epitomised by Anne (acting on the advice of her friend Lady Russell), rejecting Wentworth due to his inferior social and financial position. Of course, Anne regrets this when Wentworth returns from the Napoleonic Wars having amassed a fortune and with an admiral for a brother-in-law. While reflecting the importance of such things to the naval officer, this is a story that reflects contemporary society: social standing and money are everything. Other themes are examined in the naval fiction of Frederick Marryat, a contemporary of Austen. In *Mr Midshipman Easy* (1836), the title character is portrayed as holding foolish beliefs about the 'rights of man' and it takes a friendship with the former slave Mesty, now working on the lower deck of a British warship, to change his views. Here, and in Marryat's earlier work *Peter Simple* (1834), we see the navy, from one who served, as a force of good, the educator of young foolish men.

At this time inhabitants of the lower deck, like Mesty, were usually portrayed by artists in one of two ways. One was negative. George Cruikshank's depiction of British sailors in a tavern ashore, spending their money on drinking, gambling and whoring or Thomas Rowlandson's bawdy representation of *Portsmouth Point* was the exact image the general public expected to see. It was a different matter afloat; Cruikshank's *At Sea* shows the sailors relaxed, though still with drink in hand, intently listening to a salty yarn from an experienced sailor. A second, more patriotic assessment of the sailor is provided by James Gillray's *Fighting for the Dunghill – or Jack Tar settling Buonaparte*. Dating from 1798 the British sailor is shown sat atop a globe casually knocking a rather emaciated Napoleon Bonaparte over. This is the sailor as 'Jack Tar', the lovable rogue, defender of the free and champion of those oppressed by Bonaparte's dictatorship.

By the mid-to-late nineteenth century the image of the British 'Jack Tar' as the defender of the free world was well and truly established. Nowhere is this more evident than in the 1878 Gilbert and Sullivan operetta *HMS Pinafore*, which reinforced many Victorian stereotypes about the British sailor. He is brave and loyal, as Sir Joseph Porter, First Lord of the Admiralty declares: 'A British sailor is any man's equal'. The production opens with the hands singing:

> *We sail the ocean blue,*
> *And our saucy ship's a beauty;*
> *We're sober men and true,*
> *And attentive to our duty.*
> *When the balls whistle free*
> *O'er the bright blue sea,*
> *We stand to our guns all day;*

When at anchor we ride
On the Portsmouth tide,
We have plenty of time to play.

The actual nature of the last line is hinted at by the arrival of Little Buttercup. She is selling her varied wares, ribbons, snuff, watches:

Hail, men-o'-war's men – safeguards of your nation
Here is an end, at last, of all privation;
You've got your pay – spare all you can afford
To welcome Little Buttercup on board.

There is something fruity with the hint that underneath her 'round and rosy' exterior there could be something else for sale, as recognised by the appropriately named Dick Deadeye who has 'thought it often'. While all this saucy nonsense was perfect for the Victorians, the twentieth-century audience – in particular the United States – demanded something more.

With the advent of popular film in the 1920s and '30s Hollywood looked to the Western Front of the First World War or the new and exciting technology of the aircraft for inspiration for war films. That was until the 1935 version of *Mutiny on the Bounty* portrayed Captain William Bligh as a brutal, sadistic captain. Casting reinforced the unhistorical tone of the production with veteran horror actor Charles Laughton playing Bligh and Fletcher Christian played by 1930s' Hollywood heartthrob Clark Gable. It was during the interwar years that C.S. Forester began his series of novels about Horatio Hornblower, thereby setting the tone for modern naval fiction writing.

During the wars of the twentieth century the sailor was portrayed as a true heir to the Nelsonic tradition of duty to one's country above all other considerations. The image of the great admiral sacrificing himself for the greater good was a powerful message. It is no surprise *That Hamilton Woman* (1941), with Nelson, played by Laurence Olivier, leaving the obvious charms of Emma Hamilton (Vivien Leigh) in order to beat the French and Spanish fleet was reputedly Winston Churchill's favourite film. The film version of *In Which We Serve* (1942) was so authentic in portraying the Royal Navy that the Admiralty used it to give a flavour of naval life to new recruits. Again, the emphasis was on doing one's duty. The crew perform well under fire but 'One, however, did not' and ran from his post. This young and inexperienced sailor is forgiven, as the captain blames himself for not fully explaining the concept of duty; suitably redeemed, the sailor feels ashamed of his actions. All this was perfect, stirring stuff for a wartime audience.

After the Second World War there was a distinct split between attitudes to the conflict in Britain and the United States. In Britain the post-war years were hard (rationing continued into the 1950s), a feeling reflected in the works of Royal Navy veterans Nicholas Monsarrat, whose 1951 novel *The Cruel Sea* was turned into a successful film in 1953, and Douglas Reeman. Such works presented a realistic and gritty interpretation of the war, again emphasising the importance of duty, sacrifice and highlighting the hardships endured. Such themes were also present on the big screen in the films *Above us the Waves* (1955) and the historical classic *Sink the Bismarck!* (1960).

On radio a different picture was emerging. The radio comedy shows of the 1950s and 1960s drew upon a general awareness of naval and military slang due to increased service levels during the Second World War. In *The Goon Show*, Spike Milligan and Peter Sellers circumvented strict BBC guidelines on the use of inappropriate words by liberal use of slang terms to the utter ignorance of BBC bosses. The baton was taken up manfully by Barry Took and Marty Feldman when writing for Kenneth William's character Rambling Syd Rumpole from *Round the Horne* (1965–68). Rumpole's weekly spot consisted of a meaningless ditty alluding to all sorts of shenanigans delivered in a thick Somerset accent. Here is a prime example interspersed with real naval terminology:

> *What shall we do with a drunken nurker?*
> *Hit him in the nadgers with the bosun's plunger ... till his bodgers dangle.*

The Navy Lark, set aboard the fictional HMS *Troutbridge*, starring Leslie Phillips and Jon Pertwee, was in part based on Pertwee's own war experiences. He worked in Naval Intelligence and had been a crew member of HMS *Hood*, fortunately being transferred before her doomed final voyage in 1941. He had also worked on the naval radio show HMS *Waterlogged* in 1946. Between 1959 and 1977, 250 episodes of *The Navy Lark* were aired making it the longest-running comedy radio show. In true sailor fashion Pertwee once got so drunk on a run ashore he woke up with the tattoo of a cobra on his right forearm – this is visible in two of his outings as the Timelord *Dr Who*: *Doctor Who and the Silurians* and *Spearhead from Space!*

Across the pond, in the post-war years the mood was more celebratory, with sailors embarking on jaunts ashore and seeking romantic involvement in the musicals *On the Town* (1949) and *South Pacific* (1958). A different approach harked back to the swashbuckling escapist fun of the pre-war years in the 1951 adaption of Forester's novels of *Captain Horatio Hornblower*, starring Gregory Peck in the title role. Yet there was a darker underbelly to the American naval experience as aptly described by Herman Wouk in *The Caine Mutiny*, published in 1951. The 1954 film version with Humphrey Bogart playing Lieutenant Commander Queeg is a true classic. Queeg becomes increasingly paranoid about his role, for good reason as his crew are plotting against him, and Queeg is mutinously relieved of his command. While unhistorical, it nevertheless portrays a different navy and a different version of the war, one in which ambitious individuals put their own interests before duty, one in which the mental stress of war can cause men to break and one in which not everything goes according to plan. Such themes were also at the centre of Commander Edward Beach's 1955 novel *Run Silent, Run Deep*. Loosely based on the book of the same name, the 1958 film charts Commander Richardson's (portrayed by Clark Gable) Captain Ahab-style descent into madness in an obsessive quest to sink a Japanese destroyer. It is a quest that endangers the entire crew of Richardson's submarine and eventually costs him his life.

In the late 1960s and 1970s big budgets led to big-screen epics concentrating on the big story rather than the nuts and bolts of naval life, *Tora! Tora! Tora!* (1970) and *Midway* (1976) being the most obvious examples. Again, they showed a stylised version of naval life. Things were, however, changing. Jack Nicholson's character Billy 'Badass' Buddusky in the 1973 film *The Last Detail*, adapted from Darryl Ponsican's 1971 book, was more representative of the US Navy experience at this time. Buddusky likes drinking and whoring, hates officers and officialdom and expresses his views and feelings in coarse, unadulterated language. For example: 'Well, kid, there's more things in this life than you can possibly imagine. I knew a whore once in Wilmington. She had a glass eye. Used to take it out and wink people off for a dollar.' *The Last Detail* portrayed the navy from the bottom up, Buddusky's philosophising reflecting the thoughts of many from the lower deck. It was a world completely alien to many Americans who were more used to seeing sailors portrayed as doing their patriotic duty or as jovial characters in the rather tame productions of the post-war period. Something else happened at this time: audiences got a viewpoint from the German perspective in the gritty reality of Wolfgang Petersen's *Das Boot* (1981). Based on the 1971 book by Lothar-Günther Buchheim, which drew upon his autobiographical experiences of serving on *U-96* to present a fictionalised account, Petersen's film presented Germans as ordinary human beings doing their duty to country and comrades in time of war. Its slow-burning success also prompted another wave of submarine films, albeit the most successful of these were set against the background of the Cold War: *The Hunt for Red October* (1990) or in *Crimson Tide* (1995), the break-up of the Soviet Union.

At the same time as Ponsican and Buchheim were writing, two authors were taking naval fiction down a different path. Writing under the pen name Alexander Kent, Douglas Reeman turned his hand to Napoleonic naval warfare in his acclaimed Richard Bolitho series of novels, the first of which, *To Glory We Steer* appeared in 1968. Meanwhile, in southern France a writer was (quite literally) putting pen to paper on a project that would completely eclipse Bolitho. Patrick O'Brian's series of novels charted the careers and adventures of Captain Jack Aubrey and Dr Stephen Maturin. Like the Bolitho series they successfully captured the language and customs of the sea, bringing the world of sailing warships to life once more. The resurgence of naval fiction set the scene for the big-budget television adaption of C.S. Forester's *Horatio Hornblower*. Starring Ioan Gruffudd in the title role, eight movie-length adventures were filmed and aired between 1998 and 2003; the series won three Emmy Awards in 1999. Such success provided fertile ground for the Oscar-winning 2003 film *Master and Commander: The Far side of the World* starring Russell Crowe and loosely based on two volumes from O'Brian's series – and rumours still persist that there will be a another Jack Aubrey film.

FURTHER READING

This book has drawn examples from a wide variety of sources and covered naval history ranging from the Phoenicians right up to the present day. What follows can be no more than a general guide to sources the reader might find useful, with some additional works to add depth. I have also limited this guide to books that are readily accessible.

The most comprehensive book on naval slang is Rick Jolly's *Jackspeak: A Guide to British Naval Slang* (Maritime Books, 2000). Containing over 4,000 terms Jolly's book is an invaluable starting point; organised in an A-Z format it covers an immense breadth of subjects. While compiling such a work is a commendable exercise, the majority of the terms are not used ashore and hence there is not much in the book for those with little or no direct experience of the navy. In similar fashion, the work of Commander Covey Crump in compiling a dictionary of naval slang in the mid-1950s, while of interest, is again mainly aimed at those with a background in the senior service. It is accessed through the Royal Navy's website at www.royal-navy.mod.uk. Admiral Smyth's *Sailors Word-Book* (Conway, 2005) is a huge digest of nautical terms, and although a little dated (the original was published in 1867) is still invaluable for the subject.

Two books can be used to put a little more flesh on the bones. In Olivia Isil's *When a Loose Cannon Flogs a Dead Horse There's the Devil to Pay: Seafaring Words in Everyday Speech* (International Marine, 1996), a select number of words and phrases are presented alphabetically with some explanation as to the possible origins. The title sums up the approach taken, it is both informal and informed, if a little unsatisfying. More useful is Peter Jeans' *Ship to Shore: A Dictionary of Everyday Words and Phrases Derived from the Sea* (McGraw-Hill Professional, 2004). With over 1,300 entries arranged alphabetically it is more comprehensive that Isil's, and Jeans' use of fictional dialogue to contextualise colloquial expressions is certainly useful, but overall it suffers from similar problems, and the very breadth precludes in-depth examination of all but a few topics. All of the above works are useful but are ultimately unfulfilling, the lack of overall context gives little insight into the life of the sailor and the A-Z format make them useful works of reference but not particularly great reads.

Of the general histories of man's interaction with the sea *The History of the Ship: The Comprehensive Story of Seafaring from the Earliest Times to the Present Day* by Richard Woodman (Conway, 2002) provides a comprehensive and lucid introduction to some of the major themes. To which can be added *The Oxford Companion to Ships and the Sea* (Oxford, 2006) edited by I.C.B. Dear and Peter Kemp. On the technicalities of seafaring John Harland's *Seamanship in the Age of Sail* (Conway, 1984) has yet to be surpassed.

Regarding the British experience N.A.M. Rodger's *The Safeguard of the Sea* (HarperCollins, 1997) and *The Command of the Ocean* (Allen Lane, 2004) will, when the final volume is added, provide the most complete history of seapower in the British Isles. For the classic age of sail, Brian Lavery's *Nelson's Navy* (Conway, 1988) is still the best place to start while *The Royal Navy Since 1815* (Palgrave Macmillan, 2005) by Eric Grove is fairly self explanatory. Richard Harding's, *The Evolution of the Sailing Navy 1509–1815* (Macmillan, 1995) and Andrew Lambert's *War at Sea in the Age of Sail* (Cassell, 2002) will provide a more international feel.

Moving into the twentieth century *The Imperial War Museum Book of The War at Sea, 1914–1918* (Pan Macmillan, 2005) by Julian Thompson provides a wealth of eyewitness accounts of the Royal Navy's experience of the First World War. Max Arthur's *Lost Voices of the Royal Navy* (Hodder, 2005) provides eyewitness accounts from both World Wars. Lavery's *Churchill's Navy* (Conway, 2006) does a similar job to his *Nelson's Navy* but for the Second World War. *Conway's The War at Sea in Photographs, 1939-1945* (Conway, 2007) by Stuart Robertson and Stephen Dent provides international coverage. For the Falklands Sandy Woodward's *One Hundred Days* (HarperCollins, 2003) is ideal.

A slightly more American-centric study of naval power is provided by *At War at Sea: Naval Warfare in the Twentieth Century* by Ronald Spector (Penguin, 2002), to which *A Sailor's History of the U.S. Navy*, by Thomas Cutler (NIP, 2004) will add a human element.

Regarding specific subjects, David Cordingly provides two books on minor, but interesting, subjects. *Heroines and Harlots* (Pan, 2002) looks at women and their relationship with sailors, while *Under the Black Flag* (Random House, 2006) provides a comprehensive account of piracy. *Feeding Nelson's Navy: The True Story of Food at Sea in the Georgian Era* (Chatham, 2004) by Janet Macdonald and *Nelson's Blood: The Story of Naval Rum* (NIP, 1996) by James Pack will provide a good starting point on food and drink.

USEFUL WEBSITES

National Maritime Museum, Greenwich – www.nmm.ac.uk
The Royal Naval Museum, Portsmouth – www.royalnavalmuseum.org
Royal Navy Submarine Museum, Gosport – www.rnsubmus.co.uk
Fleet Air Arm Museum, Yeovilton – www.fleetairarm.com
Imperial War Museum – www.iwm.org.uk
US Navy Museum, Washington Navy Yard – www.history.navy.mil
HMS Victory – www.hms-victory.com
HMS Warrior – www.hmswarrior.org
HMS Belfast – hmsbelfast.iwm.org.uk
USS Constitution – www.ussconstitution.navy.mil
USS Missouri – www.ussmissouri.com
World Ship Trust – www.worldshiptrust.org
UK National Historic Ships – www.nhsc.org.uk

INDEX